CW01590211

CHESHIRE VOL II

Edited by Chris Hallam

First published in Great Britain in 2003 by
YOUNG WRITERS
Remus House,
Coltsfoot Drive,
Peterborough, PE2 9JX
Telephone (01733) 890066

All Rights Reserved

Copyright Contributors 2002

HB ISBN 0 75434 227 1
SB ISBN 0 75434 228 X

FOREWORD

This year, the Young Writers' The Write Stuff! competition proudly presents a showcase of the best poetic talent from over 40,000 up-and-coming writers nationwide.

Young Writers was established in 1991 and we are still successful, even in today's modern world, in promoting and encouraging the reading and writing of poetry.

The thought, effort, imagination and hard work put into each poem impressed us all, and once again, the task of selecting poems was a difficult one, but nevertheless, an enjoyable experience.

We hope you are as pleased as we are with the final selection and that you and your family continue to be entertained with *The Write Stuff! Cheshire Vol II* for many years to come.

CONTENTS

The Poems

HOME SWEET HOME

As I wake up on Saturday morn
I know what I want to do.
I sit at my computer
And play a game or two,
Home sweet home

I hear my mum from down below
Calling up to me,
'Tidy up that room of yours,
And make that bed,' says she.
Home sweet home

After lunch I play outside
And kick the ball about,
I run and jump and let off steam
I love to sing and shout.
Home sweet home

My brother comes to play with me,
Much to my delight
Until we argue on and on
And then we start to fight.
Home sweet home

When in bed I love to read
And cast my cares away
I think about my family
And having a wonderful day.
Home sweet home.

Michael Evans (11)
Abbey Gate College

THE CIRCUS

The amazing colourful circus,
Has finally come to town.
As the music starts with a rumbling drum roll,
Each act prances out into the ring.

The spectacular, juggling clown,
Juggles six balls with pride.

The strong, powerful weightlifter,
Lifts a very cheeky clown throwing tomatoes
at the ringmaster.

The wonderful, fantastic ringmaster,
Cracks his long whip as the elephants enter the ring.

The large, dancing elephants with huge feet,
Make a loud *thunder* on the sawdust-covered ground.

The great, breathtaking gymnasts,
Swizzle and dangle from the poles.

The lazy, tiresome photographer,
Takes pictures of an awesome circus.

The loudest audience around,
Applaud to an outstanding, sensational circus.

The circus has ended.
All is quiet,
But will awaken soon
To entertain another loud, applauding audience.

Jemma Fitzsimmons (11)
Hartford High School

PERFORM

The audience chat away waiting for entertainment,
One by one, all the clowns follow each other out of the tiny car,
They stand in an orderly form with their huge feet reaching the audience.
Outside the tent, the pattering of rain begins,
inside everyone is dry and warm.
The tears of laughter get everyone like the shot of a gun,
then the clowns bow.
Everyone stands and cheers them on,
The clowns scuttle back in the car and they drive off with the sound of the horn beeping every 10 seconds.
The rain begins to fade.
Everybody stands and makes their way home through the puddles,
all they know is that they will be there again because the circus
is back and ready to perform!

Jordan Kettle (11)
Hartford High School

THE ROAR OF THE RING TOP

The roar of the ring top brightens up the night,
The funny circus clowns are inside running around and pretending to fight.
The strongman is in the ring burning his muscles and using his might.
As well, the audience is bewildered at this sight.
The trapeze artists are at the top ready for their flight.
As people yawn and fall asleep, it's a good end to a great night.

Jack Patten (12)
Hartford High School

The Circus

I walk into the tent,
Hearing the cheer of the crowd,
As I walk to my seat I smell the popcorn,
I see the dancing horses waiting to start.

I sit down in my seat,
I watch the clowns juggle.
I eat my candyfloss,
While I listen to the jokes the clowns make.

Next, it's the trapeze artists
I see them swing up high, all the way to the top,
I hear the gasps of the audience,
As they watch the acrobats flip.

The show is over,
I walk out,
The smell of the food fades away,
The cheer of the crowd has gone,
The circus is finally over.

Chloe Walker
Hartford High School

The Circus

The laughing prancing clown
Runs around the giant ring.
To the very loud roar of the laughing audience.
Outside the big top the hot sun rules the sky.
Inside the noisy big top are the children and adults.
Screams and laughter, the circus has finally come to town.

Samantha Ann Sanders (11)
Hartford High School

THE BULLY

I take the dreaded walk to school
where everybody hates me.
There awaits the king of bullies
and he leads his thugs into a line.

The day at school is worse than ever
but they aren't really that clever.
They wait for me behind the wall
but I can see that the ship has sailed.

It even continues after school
when you thought they wouldn't.
They're probably jealous of my capabilities.
They bully to make them look tough.

I dread every Monday morn
and drag myself to the so-called prison.
Again they wait and wait and wait
because they start when the teachers can't see.

Shaun Mattock (12)
Hartford High School

THE CIRCUS

The hooves of the thundering horses amaze the roaring audience.
The juggling funny clowns make all the children laugh.
The acrobats make everyone say, 'Wow!'
Outside, the sky becomes as dark as night can be.
'The circus has come to town,' say the people when they
go out eating and drinking.

Charlotte Anne Casey (11)
Hartford High School

CLOWN POEM

C racking jokes, throwing pies around the ring.
L aughing loudly and dancing around the ring.
O utside, the world so quiet, inside, roaring and laughing
of the crowd around the ring.
W hirling a ball on one finger making the crowd cheer.
N ow the end, when he rides on a unicycle along the wire
and the crowd does a Mexican wave.

Christopher Cain (11)
Hartford High School

THE BIG TOP CIRCUS

C lowns, lions, jugglers and trapeze
I nside the big top the crowds get teased
R oaring lions and the cracking whips
C lowns, jumping, dancing and doing tricks
U mbrellas, water, horns and balls
S tep inside for fun and laughter like
you've never seen before.

Samuel Tours (11)
Hartford High School

CIRCUS

C lowns juggling and laughing.
I in the big top, the smell of doughnuts.
R oadshow back in town.
C ircuses travel all around.
U nder the big top you have a good laugh.
S nakes wrap around people's necks.

Robert Garner (12)
Hartford High School

BULLIES

B rat, he acts like an enormous brat.
U gly, a bully is always ugly.
L ethargic, most of the time they are lazy.
L ively, they are sometimes lively and awake.
I gnorant, he is ignorant and self-centred
E nvious, he is envious of other people
that is why he wants to bully them.
S how-off, most of they time they are show-offs,
they do this to get attention.

Jonathon De Sousa (12)
Hartford High School

BULLY

B ullies try to hurt you
U sually they steal from you
L ike yourself, they get bullied too. They
L ike seeing you hurt.
I f a bully hurts you, tell a teacher or a friend
E nd this fight.
S chool should not be hard.

Jordan Parker (12)
Hartford High School

BULLY

B uying time to save yourself,
U ndescribably miserable,
L oser,
L ooking for danger and backing away,
Y ou are scared of going out of the house.

Sarah Gerrard (12)
Hartford High School

BULLY

My bully is a coward, he's evil, he's scary.
He's jealous of me,
He's envious of me,
All he wants to do is make a fool of me,
That's the bully that I have.

My bully is a chicken, he's scared, he's a thug.
He's boastful and a show-off,
He's threatening and frightening,
And he is self-centred.
That's the bully that I have.

I guess it's his bad background,
Not many people think he's a wimp,
I know he's jealous,
But I don't blame him,
That's the bully that I have.

Adam Sambell (12)
Hartford High School

THE CIRCUS

Creepy clowns squashing their faces
into a tremendous smile!
Trumpeting elephants parading across the ring.

The roaring lions in the cages.
The ringmaster taming his employees
with his deadly snapping whip,
and the beautiful smell of popcorn
streaming up your nose.

Jack Hayes (11)
Hartford High School

BULLIES

Bullies are mean
And not very clean,
They're not very bright
And they're hardly right.

They hit you here
And bring a tear
To your little face
With a very big pace.

They'll take all your lunch,
With their little bunch
They act very bad
And make your life sad.

They will always blame you
And laugh at you too,
But remember to tell
Before the bell
And be happy once again.

Hannah Robinson (12)
Hartford High School

TRAPEZE ARTISTS

The trapeze artists,
Spiralling out of control,
In the spectacular circus ring,
On a cold winter's night,
To magically entertain the excited crowd.
A dazzling display performed by the artists.

Mhairi Gilmour (11)
Hartford High School

BULLIES

B ullies are evil and envious
U ndermining people all the time
L oving to hurt people
L oving to make them cry
Y oung people always get hit.

V ery scared people
I n the dark they keep this bullying
C autious all the time
T o hide is all they can do
I n a crowd they hide it
M oaning and groaning from the pain.

Sarah Jones (13)
Hartford High School

THE BULLIES

A bully may be threatening,
Or maybe even frightening,
But deep down they are scared,
A bully may bc teasing,
And can be deceiving,
But deep down they're a coward,
A bully may be evil,
And sometimes can be boastful,
But deep down they are jealous,
Just remember,
Every bully has a weakness,
Even though they may not show it!

Cherylyn Bennett (12)
Hartford High School

Bullying

B ackstabbing evil menace.
U sually he's scared or jealous.
L ooking around every corner in fear.
L ying in wait for you
Y ou cannot escape.
I n your head and mind you're scared.
N ever try and fight back.
G onna get him in the end.

Scott Fishwick (12)
Hartford High School

The Circus

C lowns are funny
I n the circus that comes to town,
R eal ladies and gentleman watch,
C aring for the animals
U nder the big top the bands sing.
S haring and stroking the animals.
The clown has left town.

Hannah Fallows (11)
Hartford High School

Bully Poem

B ig, bad boys, bully boys,
U gly, underhand.
L ame, lying lunatics.
L ittle losers.
Y elling yobs.

Martyn East (12)
Hartford High School

The Circus

C ircus, yes! We are going to the circus today and I can't wait.

I t has clowns that dance around the noisy ring.

R unning round and round are the horses making a clicking sound,
now the noise is getting worse.

C hildren laugh inside because the clowns are juggling
and falling off their unicycles.

U nderneath the big top, madness is coming along.

S pectacular is the circus, you really ought to go some day.

Vicky Cadman (11)
Hartford High School

Bullies

Bullies are mean, evil, self-centred and are gimps.
They think they're so cool but really they are wimps.
They threaten you so you get upset!
But they have been bullied once, I bet!

They are boastful chickens with bad backgrounds.
Their own schools are probably out of bounds.
They are jealous, stupid and mean.
There are parts of the world they haven't seen.

One day in their life they will look back at the past
And think, 'Oh my goodness, how did I last?'

Stephanie Eyes (12)
Hartford High School

Cry

Cry when the bully at your school smacks you in the face
Cry when you walk past them, they laugh and sneer at you.
Cry when you get a question wrong in class and everyone
looks at you like you're thick.
Don't listen, for there's no need to cry.
Tell a teacher or parent, don't let them attack you,
Don't be stupid, be sensible.

Lucinda Firman (12)
Hartford High School

The Circus

Inside the stripy big top, the crowd was going wild,
The band were playing loudly, the animals were dancing,
Then the band stopped playing,
The spotlight shone over the crowd onto the stage,
The man on the stage gave us a big welcome,
Then the band started playing again.

Nicola Davies (11)
Hartford High School

The Circus

The falling, bawling, laughing clown,
Skips and bobs around the ring,
To the excited audience, laughing and clapping,
In the dark night, lit with shiny stars.

Charlotte Howard (11)
Hartford High School

BULLY POEM

There are many words to describe a bully,
Here are just a few,
Jealous, mean, always boasting,
Telling you you're thick.
They think they're perfect,
That they're the best,
Make you feel unwanted,
They're envious, evil, wimps, all thugs,
Trying to make you feel sad.
Scary, coward, show-off, self-centred,
Thinking you're the chicken.
Evil, thug, teasing, mad,
But when it comes to class, a turn,
They're suddenly an angel!
When you tell the teacher,
She won't believe you,
You feel as small as can be
But finally home,
The best part of the day.

Yvette Burrell (12)
Hartford High School

THE CIRCUS

The lashing lion tamer
Launches his whip,
On the roaring lions.
Outside the glittering stars
Shine in the night sky,
Inside, children enjoy,
As the circus will leave tomorrow.

Sam Pimlott (12)
Hartford High School

FEELINGS

Shock
Boat shaking
Eyes crying
Wind blowing
Anger starting
Heart pounding

Miserable
Eyes staring
Feet walking
Tears spilling
Fists clenching
Mind exploding.

Shock!

Lisa Bailey (11)
Henbury High School

ANGER

Bad
blood boiling
hopes falling
pots smashing
pride crashing
dreams breaking
brain shaking
fist grasping
head rasping
pulse rising
tears dying
hopes climbing.

David Graham (11)
Henbury High School

WHERE?

Scared!
Heart pounding.
Mind thinking.
Fingers scratching.
Feet pounding.
Eyes popping.
Body shaking.

Calm.
Muscles relaxing.
Nerves calming.
Panic subsiding.
Pain leaving.
Brain wondering.
Heart beating.

Dewi Chappell (11)
Henbury High School

POEM

Anger meeting
Eyes stinging
Legs failing
Body cooling
Lungs blocking
Teeth aching
Voice going
Hope fading
Storm dying
Grin forming
Brother hurting.

James Behan
Henbury High School

FEELINGS

Rage
Lights vanishing
Tears dripping
Heart pounding
Hands waving
Hope seeping

Fear
Water freezing
Ball slipping
Head bobbing
Legs kicking
Ship shrinking

Anger

Miles Holt (11)
Henbury High School

ANGER!

Fist pounding
Blood rushing
Feet banging
Tears pouring
Teeth flying
Head busting
Brain exploding
Eyes blaring
Stomach aching
Head whizzing
Finally stopping
Pain disappearing!

Chris Bailey (11)
Henbury High School

The Haunted House

Coiling pebbles, winding up the narrow sinuous path.
Bright lights of the house,
Flashing as the thunder roars.
Thick fog swamping the brisk, dead grass.
Dusty, old graves, standing dull and bold,
The names fading away slowly.

My hair blowing in the misty breeze,
Creaking sounds, as the doors in the house open.
The rusty door hands,
Twist round and round.
The curtains swaying,
The floorboards creaking.
The cobwebs glistening in the moonlight.
The letterbox bolted shut,
With old wood and nails.
The old house stands,
Looking haunted and scary.

Kim McGahey (13)
Henbury High School

A Place I Know

I wander through the cold, dull, damp school
Its walls encase souls.
The corridors crowded, then suddenly silent.
Echoing large halls.

The smell of rotten school food.
The bickering of pupils.
The screeching of teachers howling at their students.
The ringing of the bell through the corridors.

I see ill-painted walls
Chudy in the cracks
The large crush hall with creaky wooden floors
where assemblies are held.
The long desolate corridors.

Jonathan Parker
Henbury High School

SCHOOL!

As I walk through the long blue doors
I hear the sound of strictness.

As I walk up the steep brown stairs
it's dull and tiring.

I walk into my classroom and see
marks of weakness,
marks of woe.

In every voice of every sound
I hear the tiredness of boring hard work.

As the bell rings, it's very loud
and it's real hubbub.

As the day slowly goes by
all the students write their homework
energetically with their pens.

As everybody leaves the long blue doors
the strictness sound disappears.

Kylie Cox (13)
Henbury High School

Feelings

Rage
Feet jumping.
Glass breaking.
Blood rushing.
Fist thumping.
Tears stinging.

Fade
Ship fading.
Hope dying.
Life ending.
Heart stopping.
Eyes overflowing.

Rage
Head banging.
Teeth chattering.
Stomach aching.
Legs aching.
Body shaking.

Natalie Joanne O'Brien (11)
Henbury High School

Anxiety

Anxiety
Heart thumping
Stomach turning
Blood rushing
Mind sinking
Throat paralysing

Fear
Hopes falling
Life taking
Waves clashing
Feet working
Heart jumping

Anxiety!

Sabine Grimshaw
Henbury High School

A Poem On A Place I Know

The grass is damp and foliage near,
With the eerie shadows cast by the moon,
Cars and birds are all you hear,
With the dim glow of the streetlight.

A bird takes flight, it is unexpected,
Not knowing what it was I did, but I can't move,
I see a silhouette of that bird; a torch is all I want,
I go on, moist ankles, dewy grass.

Startled by a low bush,
I nearly hit the floor,
I continue cautiously yet still not in a rush,
The river is getting louder along with all of that.

Someone is behind me, who the heck is that?
Not watching where I'm going, I trip and fall down
It's just my friend, he's not all that,
Dark clothes are all I can make out.

John Barnes (13)
Henbury High School

ANGER/DRAINING

Anger

Eyes shrinking
Voice shouting
Fists clenching
Blood pounding
Arms flailing
Muscles tightening

Draining

Head spinning
Pulse slowing
Muscles relaxing
Fists loosening
Eyes opening
Voice stopping.

James Wilson (11)
Henbury High School

ANGRY

Annoyed
Bad temper
Enraged
Door slamming
Neck breaking
Heart pounding
Pulse racing
Tempers flaring.

Daniel Roberts (11)
Henbury High School

FEELINGS

Provoking
Blood spluttering
Temperature rising
Fists gasping
Muscles heaving
Head whirling
Eyeballs rolling
Teeth grinding
Eyebrows frowning.

Crying
Tears flowing
Eyes weeping
Nose running
Heart swelling.

Lee Scott
Henbury High School

RAGE

Feet stamping
Doors banging
Me frowning
Body shaking
Hands pushing
Head bursting
Brain cracking
Objects flying
Heart pounding
Mouth fizzing
Fists throwing.

I'm raging!

Emma Rutherford (11)
Henbury High School

FEELINGS

Erupting
Teeth gritting
Eyes blazing
Bruises invading
Blood flying
Things smashing
Heads banging
Pulse rising

Draining
Heart swelling
Eyes flooding
Stomach aching
Anger shrinking
Screams draining.

Chris Birch
Henbury High School

FEELINGS

Terror
Bone chilling
Body plunging
Heart stopping
Horror rising

Hope
Life descending
Tears flooding
Death nearing
Soul surrendering

Terror!

Ellen Taylor (11)
Henbury High School

FEELINGS

Anger
Teeth gritting
Hate bubbling
Fists clenching
Head pounding
Glass shattering.

Hope
Tears showing
Heart slowing
Hope fighting
Mouth smiling
Eyes sparkling
Teeth showing.

Becky Walker (11)
Henbury High School

FEELINGS

Anger
Eyes swelling
Heart pounding
Body trembling
Tears building
Rage towering

Sadness
Heart sinking
Life collapsing
Feet stomping
Tears rolling

Anger!

Stephanie Lauren Bracegirdle (11)
Henbury High School

Kensuke's Kingdom

Pain!
Jellyfish stinging
Pain searing
Body throbbing
Heart hurting
Legs kicking

Sore!
Electric shocking
Agony excruciating
Muscles dying
Voice screeching
Mind losing

Pain!

Zack Hall (11)
Henbury High School

Feelings

Fury
Head smashing
Legs crashing
Hand clapping
Teeth changing

Anger
Fists thumping
Legs kicking
Head butting
Eyes glaring.

Alex Worthington (11)
Henbury High School

FEELINGS

Anger
Feet stomping
Tears splashing
Leaves crackling
Sticks smashing
Hearts pounding

Anger
Wind clashing
Hopes failing
Eyes staring
Voices blaring
Heads pounding

Anger!

Liam Macdonald (12)
Henbury High School

FEELINGS

Pain
Feet splashing
Arms waving
Neck aching
Legs stinging
Hands wrinkling.

Fate
Life fading
Eyes closing
Soul sinking
Mind moping
Jellyfish stinging.

Alex Ferguson (11)
Henbury High School

Scared

Scared
Waves crashing
Body chilling
Mind sinking
Tear spilling
Mouth filling

Pain
Leg tiring
Heart beating
Eye closing
Life threatening
Hope killing

Scared.

Bryony Ward (11)
Henbury High School

Feelings Poem

Horror
Heart thumping
Hope fading
Bones shaking
Blood pumping
Tears falling.

Shock
Pulse racing
Mind exploding
Boat swaying
Helicopter searching
Coastguard coming.

Karen Hunt (11)
Henbury High School

MICHAEL AND KENSUKE'S FEELINGS

Betrayed

Feet crushing
Teeth grinding
Heart sinking
Eyes crossing
Head shaking

Sorrow

Hurt crashing
Stomach turning
Revenge coming
Fear striking
Sorry fading.

Alice Newton (11)
Henbury High School

FEELINGS

Betrayal.
Fire blazing.
Heart pounding.
Tears coming.
Emotions exploding.
Leaves burning.

Hurt.
Heart breaking.
Emotions filling.
Rage building.
Temper rising.
Anger overflowing.
Betrayal.

Lorna McKillop (11)
Henbury High School

Feelings

Hope

Mind racing
Thoughts chasing
Hope rising
Face smiling
Body exciting

Glass breaking
Smoke coming
Leaves crackling
Face burning
Man stamping

Hope,

Sam Houghton (11)
Henbury High School

Poem

I'm saved
Hands waving
Legs springing
Fire burning
Feet stamping
Kensuke.

Rage
Sand flying
Smoke burning
Boat disappearing
Kensuke shouting
Rage.

Leanne McClean (11)
Henbury High School

FEELINGS

Fear
Waves crashing
Arms waving
Head sinking
Water splashing
Voice yelling

Pain
Foot stinging
Voice yelping
Back aching
Jellyfish chasing
Daylight fading

Fear.

Marc Furness (11)
Henbury High School

ANGER

Fury
Anger burning
Arms flailing
Heart pounding
Fists shaking
Despair
Depression seeping
Sadness swelling
Adrenalin calming
Head spinning
Fury.

Sarah Wilson (11)
Henbury High School

Sea Dream

Shiny, sparkling, shimmering,
A happy place,
Blue, through green and grey.
Sea eagle searches for his prey.

Crash, crash,
Grinding of the rocks,
White horses dancing
And prancing.

A sailing ship I see,
Sitting upon the sea,
Fish playing round the bow,
Dipping and diving, dipping and diving.

As I look back on the sea,
Big and blue it is,
Smaller, smaller, smaller,
Gone . . .

Matthew Lamb (14)
Henbury High School

The Cellar

I walk down the sinuous stairs
All alone in the dark
I feel around for the light switch
Running my hands along the cold brick walls.

The light is flickering
In the misty background
The cold air running past my face
My hair blowing in the breeze.

The water dripping
From the leaky tap
Mice and rats
Crawling from the gap.

Chloe Taylor (13)
Henbury High School

WOODS!

The dangerous animal yowls,
It waits to tear your flesh from your bones
Like a cannibal
Waiting to foul.

I hear a sound
Of dangerous wolves
Stamping around on the old leaves,
All I hear are wolves walking around.

Seeing the dark floor
And all the shady trees,
Everything looks so sad here.
I can see a wooden hut with a dark black door.

I can see the bright sunset
Rising over the hills,
It's beautiful
But it is very wet.

Scott Wilkinson
Henbury High School

Wrong Feelings

Wrong

Heart pounding
Head banging
Bloodstream thrashing
Fists raging
Arms killing

Feelings

Eyes flooding
Pride seeping
Hope smearing
Completion fading
Heart sinking

Daniel Jones (12)
Henbury High School

Feelings

Pain

Body stinging
Voice screaming
Boy gasping.

Hope

Ship approaching
Desperate yelling
Hope fading
Ship's gone.

Pain!

Joe Tonge (11)
Henbury High School

FEELINGS

Pain

Limb stinging
Muscle stiffening
Lungs filling
Body sinking
Neck burning

Anger

Stick waving
Body shaking
Mouth shouting
Eye twitching
Side stitching

Fear.

Josh Wayles (12)
Henbury High School

FOREBODING

Legs collapsing
Feet stamping
Brain bashing
Head banging
Eyes popping
Ears steaming
Heart sweating
Nose twitching
Hair blowing
Teeth tightening
Tongue panting
Bones breaking
Tears emerging

Jack Millward
Henbury High School

SCHOOL

I walk through every dark corridor
Near where the outside world carries on
And ignore everyone I meet
Faces full of fear, faces full of woe

The loud and scary bell
Children screaming not to make them stay
Every teacher's loud and booming voice
The non-existent cries of joy are lost.

Dark and dreary rooms bring your fears to life
While Mr Dillon cuddles up to his ugly wife
Teachers all grouped round
With faces like bad weather

Everyone wishes to come here
They even use a wishing well
Parents think it's Heaven,
But believe me, it's Hell!

Aimée Howard (13)
Henbury High School

SCHOOL

As you walk down the dirty paths,
You hear students chatting away.
You see students running around
And you see littered floors.

You hear students calling each other.
You hear teachers shouting.
You hear doors slamming.
You hear things dropping on the floor.

You see ripped posters.
You see walls that haven't been painted.
You see broken windows.
You see dirty floors.

You can smell sweaty feet.
You can smell food ready for break.
You can smell damp.
You can smell the boys' changing rooms.

Laura Hamand (13)
Henbury High School

A Place I Know

This place I know is nice and cosy
The warmth from the fire makes my cheeks rosy.
The carpet's soft under my feet
I smile when my family and I greet.

I hear my family together
I heard the rain if it's bad weather.
The radio's playing in the background
In my room I can't hear a sound.

I see the cushions all soft and fluffed up.
I see the table and on top is a cup.
When I see my bed I want to sleep
When I get down the stairs I take a leap.

I go into the kitchen to get a drink
As I walk along the carpet, my feet sink
I go outside to see my bunny
Sometimes he does things that are very funny.

Azita Zadeh
Henbury High School

ANGER

Fury
Head banging
Feet stamping
Arms shaking
Legs moving
Heart pounding
Blood racing.

Rage
Head collapsing
Feet kicking
Teeth clenching
Lungs breaking
Tears falling
Fear crashing.

Phillip Morrall (12)
Henbury High School

KENSUKE'S KINGDOM POEM

Anger
Head pounding
Arms bulging
Blood rushing
Fists clenching
Eyes filling

Hope
Heart singing
Brain thinking
Eyes shining
Face rising.

Michael Dowse (11)
Henbury High School

School

Oh no! It's time for school.
First it's tech:
Bake a cake!
Now it's music:
Time to play or pay!
At last it's break; time to rest!
It's PE:
Got to show how far you can throw!
Good, it's lunch:
Time to munch!
Now for art, *silence!*
I have to draw a boar!
Last, it's maths:
PI! I'd rather die!
Ahhh! Home time;
That's it for today.

Marcus Cronin (12)
Holmes Chapel Comprehensive School

I Have A Pony

I have a pony,
All of my own,
So has Tony,
But he's a roan,
Mine is a black one,
With such a long mane,
So let's have a gallop,
Right down the lane.

Sharna Wilson (12)
Holmes Chapel Comprehensive School

WEATHER

Thunder is a roaring giant,
His voice booming down like a round of drums,
Crashing, rumbling around splitting the sky.

Rain is like a hammer pounding down on a cold, dark day,
Bouncing off windows and doors,
Pattering like little children's feet.

Lightning is like a sharp tongue lashing down,
A line of light through a sea of grey clouds,
A fork flashing and striking down on the world.

Wind is a howling dog in pain,
Whistling through trees and branches fiercely,
Blustery and strong, his anger is released.

Vicki Barratt (11)
Holmes Chapel Comprehensive School

A FUNFAIR

I rush towards the raging bull,
To see the blinding dragons,
To rush and see the pungent smells of the Minotaur
Run, run, run, run, to the raging bull.

It's fun, scary, fast, colourful, blinding, sickening,
Pungent, exciting, whizzing, whirring, sparkling,
Shimmering and *terrifying!*

It's spooky, freaky, fast and funky, let's
Run, run, run, run to the rampaging bull.

I dash out of the screeching banshee's mouth,
Laughing, laughing, laughing.

Sophie Williamson (12)
Holmes Chapel Comprehensive School

Funfair

Joy and happiness, screams and sadness.

I am laughter,
I come from the mouths of the children,
On the dancing dodgem,
Whizzing waltzers,
Rogue roller coaster.
I am a clown making a river of laughter.

I am a scream the ghost train left behind.
I am a goldfish wondering where my friends are.
I am a freak from the freak show.
People are scared of me.
I am a helter-skelter,
People sliding down my back.

Joy and happiness, screams and sadness.

Jonathan Sparks (11)
Holmes Chapel Comprehensive School

Untitled

The cheeky chicken comes on a dish or plate,
Before, the terrific tender turkey gets delivered in a crate.
Cheesy chips fry in the pan,
Where the friendly fish found its first tan.
Apple crumble, peas and potatoes,
Mixed together makes you ready to rumble.
Pink pork praises most people, at a dinner table,
Where the wonderful watery walnut wilts
with the western watermelon!

Jonathan Maddock (12)
Holmes Chapel Comprehensive School

PARTIES

I love parties.
The cakes with the Smarties
that bake in the oven.

I love parties.
The presents as big as elephants
glittering in the room.
'Open them, open them,' everyone cries.

I love parties.
The bouncing balloons all floaty like clouds
all around the big, big room, popping with a boom!

I love parties.
Lots of cards, big and small
all of the wrapping paper scrunched up in a ball.
'Bye-bye everyone, time to go.'
I love parties!

Leanne Norrey (12)
Holmes Chapel Comprehensive School

WEATHER

The weather can be like a roaring monster;
that's why I never go out in it.
The misty weather is like a pot of white paint;
like me when I am freezing cold.
The loud thunderous weather is like a huge, screaming monster;
as I am when I graze my knee.
The wet, rainy weather is like a bath of freezing cold ice cubes;
like me when I eat all the ice cream.

Hannah Eadon (11)
Holmes Chapel Comprehensive School

SEPTEMBER 11TH 2001

The plane hit the towers.
The whole world stopped.
The crash was as loud as a rocket
And it was scary as death.
People were dying in numbers.
All the firefighters went into the buildings
never to be seen again.
The heroic people saved one plane
but lost again.
People were dying in numbers.
My heart stopped.
It was sad.
I have never seen anything so bad.
People were dying in numbers!

Thomas Hall (12)
Holmes Chapel Comprehensive School

HOW BORING

How boring, there's nothing to do,
I've got to stick to my brother like glue.
How boring, I'm standing here,
Waiting for a pint of beer,
To get me up with a bit of cheer.
How boring, to sit there, to do nothing
And go nowhere.
How boring, lying here, every day,
To do nothing, or to play.
The farmers are happy but would you be too?
How boring it was to live in the countryside.
Now I'm in the big city, learning how to drive.

David Bleasdale (12)
Holmes Chapel Comprehensive School

MAGIC

So you think magic's just for kids,
Well I'll tell you a trick or two!
Abracadabra! Hocus Pocus!
Magic words, but just a few!

Not just sorcerers with bushy beards,
Or wicked witches with bold, black hats!
Or slimy slugs and fidgety frogs,
Or beastly bugs and all that!

Magical things can affect the ordinary,
They don't have to be a witch!
Funny findings have been known,
Of ludicrous lotions in a dirty ditch!

So what do you think of the 'manky magic'
Now I've told you a thing or two?
I hope you've changed your mangled mind,
Or magnificent magic will come and get you!

Emily Thompson (12)
Holmes Chapel Comprehensive School

FAVOURITE FOODS

Delicious jammy doughnuts, all you can eat,
With mouth-watering mashed potato, it will be a treat,
There will be slimy sardine sandwiches sliding down your throat,
Joyful juicy jelly that will melt in your belly
And for dessert you can have palatable pineapple pudding
That will go right to your tummy.

Charlotte Fellowes (11)
Holmes Chapel Comprehensive School

WEATHER

The sun is like a fried egg,
all yellow, hot and nothing around it.
The snow is white like on top of a
white iced cake at Christmastime.
The rain is a pain and waters us all.
Wind is like a hardbacked book.
The sun soaks up socks and shoes.
The wind wipes up walkers and worms.
The rain raids robbers on roadways.
The snow stops sidewalks and snails.
Rain is wet, sun is dry, snow is cold.
Wind is chilly. The weather is full of
wonderful things, but none like the
Wild
Wet
Surf's up dude
Tidal wave!

Natalie Latham (12)
Holmes Chapel Comprehensive School

PETS

I have nine pets,
Three dogs, three cats, one vet.
A sheep and a horse,
That will never starve,
As they are as big as balloons.
A crocodile,
With a sharp tooth smile,
Vile another to raise your bile.

Simon Adams (12)
Holmes Chapel Comprehensive School

HOCKEY

Here I am in pain, in bed
Asleep, can't move my head
Got hit with a stick
Made me unfit

In my dream
I stood and gleamed
Thinking what did this mean
Just saw myself running, cunning
With the ball.

Someone who was tall
Hit me with a stick
I lay on the ground hit
Hurting inside
It took away my pride.

I heard my parents beside me
Not full of joy.
They bought me a new toy
Children beside me were eating bread.

I had broken my leg
Lucky I hadn't cracked my head
Needed food
Unhappy because I was in a bad mood.

Fiona Drake (11)
Holmes Chapel Comprehensive School

THE ROLLER COASTER

The ride starts off slow, then here we go!
My stomach slips as the ride dips
and it churns as the tide turns.
If you look over the side,
the people look like ants looking up at you!

When you do a loop-the-loop,
all the screams start rolling in.
Then the ride is over and people feel relieved
but some people want another go.
Everyone else says, *'No!'*

Jack Baskerville (11)
Holmes Chapel Comprehensive School

Hallowe'en

Witches fly through the night
Candles in pumpkins, burning bright
Knock on the door, 'Trick or treat?'
Dressed up children with running feet.

The time is near
Witches are here
They carry their broom
There's one in the room.

They have zits
And they look like the pits
They have a long nose
And ugly-looking toes
Their skin is green
And they're very mean.

Celebrate Hallowe'en!

Sing the song all day long
Trick or treat in the street.

Celebrate Hallowe'en!

Steven Bebbington (12)
Holmes Chapel Comprehensive School

The Weather

W inter is when white glitter falls from the sky.
E aster is when the sun shines and the wind blows strong.
A utumn's brown leaves cover the footpath so it goes
crunch, crunch when touched.
T he robin's red chest sticks out in the white snow.
H ot days make you want to drink.
E veryone likes the cold, smooth snow to play in.
R ough weather can be lots of noises and can make you dull.

Nick Boon (11)
Holmes Chapel Comprehensive School

The Funfair

F amilies having lots of fun.
U p, up, up, down, down, down, on the raging roller coaster.
N ever again will I ride the ghoulish ghost train.
F lames rise from the magician's mouth.
A mazing is the running roundabout.
I really like the flashing funfair.
R unning around, lost in all the excitement.

Alex David Sheldon (11)
Holmes Chapel Comprehensive School

Cars

C ars are cool
A cceleration is the tool
R acing the roads
S creeching tyres around the bends.

Jack Ollerton (12)
Holmes Chapel Comprehensive School

Birthday

B irthdays are a time to celebrate and have fun.
I cing is layered on the lovely cake.
R eceiving cards, money and presents.
T oys are given as presents and gifts.
'H appy birthday!' is said from all your friends and family.
D ozens of presents to open.
A unties, uncles, grandmas and grandads come to visit.
Y our birthday is a special day, make sure you enjoy it,
it only comes round once a year.

Martyn Harris (12)
Holmes Chapel Comprehensive School

My Birthday

B rilliant!
I t's going to be the best day!
R aining weather doesn't ruin the fun!
T he biggest party with all my friends!
H uge presents to open!
D ancing at the disco!
A ll the party food! Another
Y ear to wait once again!

Katie Goulbourn (13)
Holmes Chapel Comprehensive School

Fire

Roaring flames burn high
Burning anything in its path
Charging through the forest.

Robert Schofield (12)
Holmes Chapel Comprehensive School

FUNFAIR

I reached the peak of the ride,
I was 400 feet above the skies!
The car was creaking at the highest height,
Whoosh! I fell through the clouds,
Further, further, further down.
A million miles a second,
The car seemed to fly,
Whoosh! I did the loop-the-loop.
I came to a halt, the adventure was over.
I staggered to a stall,
To throw a ball.
I won a small, fluffy toy.
I gave it to my brother.
He went on a carousel,
Up and down it fell.
Lower and lower, it came to a halt,
Stopped in its tracks
And we set off home.

Daniel Smith (11)
Holmes Chapel Comprehensive School

THE FUNFAIR

Boom, boom, boom, goes the busy bouncy castle
Click, click, click, goes the laughing log flume
Up, up, up on the terrifying big, big dipper
Bang, bang, bang goes the coconut shy
Up and down, up and down on the merry-go-round
Round and round goes the helter-skelter
At the funfair ground.

Mark Gamwell (11)
Holmes Chapel Comprehensive School

The Roller Coaster

Waiting in the queue
  regretting all the time.
    Then the train arrives,
      car by car,
        the queue shuffles forward
          and we get on.
            I wish I hadn't done this,
              I'm going to regret this,
              Click! Click! Click! Click!
                Up the hill we go.
                    I hate the butterflies
                      and the queasy feeling.
                        The car stops.
                    Don't look down!
                Aaarrrggghhh!
            That wasn't bad but
      I think I left my stomach behind!

Robert Flanders (11)
Holmes Chapel Comprehensive School

The Goat

Friendly and playful
white, black and coloured.
Spotty and fussy
fat and full
blarty and skinny
naughty and slow
dirty and clean
quiet and noisy.
That's what a goat is like.

Steven Symms (12)
Holmes Chapel Comprehensive School

The Midnight Feast

I crept downstairs onto the floor,
Down the hall towards the door,
I opened it like I didn't know where
Anyone was, no one was there.

I walked inside looking for the fridge,
It was like finding a non-existent bridge,
I found it in the corner of the room,
I ran towards it at full zoom.

I opened the door, the light came on,
I ate the contents, one by one,
Ham, cakes and two fruit pies,
The food glistened in my eyes.

From above I heard a knock,
I turned my head to look at the clock,
Half-past seven, I turned to lead,
I think I better get back to bed.

Matthew Kaye (12)
Holmes Chapel Comprehensive School

Weather Week

On Monday, it was as hot as walking into an oven.
On Tuesday, it tippled it down with trillions of rain.
On Wednesday the weather was wonderfully woven.
On Thursday the weather drove me insane.
On Friday the insects and birds were frozen.
On Saturday, it was misty which was a shame.
On Sunday, it was sunny and now it starts all over again!

Michael Joyce (11)
Holmes Chapel Comprehensive School

HALLOWE'EN

Little losers come to your door
When it's dark you should be scared
Because when you're in the Land of Snore
The witching hour is up in a roar.

Massive warts on their long noses
Black cats following them around
And on their broomsticks in different poses
Flying up and down and all around.

Pumpkins come to life, cats to bats
And spells which turn brothers to mats
And spells that turn hogs to hats
The moon is full and the stars twinkled at that.

When the clock strikes one, it's all over
They all creep back under your bed
And into your cupboards
But whatever you do, don't look under the covers!

Lauren Spencer (12)
Holmes Chapel Comprehensive School

APOCALYPSE

Devils dance with demons dead
And from the Hell mouth they will come.
Trashing and tormenting the human race.
Fires engulfing the entire Earth population in one foul swoop.
Those surviving are then enslaved and tortured
for the rest of their lives.

Robert Wood (12)
Holmes Chapel Comprehensive School

ROLLER COASTER RIDE

R egret,
O h no! We're moving,
L unacy,
L ingering in space,
E xcitement growing,
R attling rails,

C reaking cars,
O blivion,
A wesome drop,
S creaming faces,
T aut with terror,
E ventually we stop,
R elief, I'm still alive!

Rosie Gibbons (11)
Holmes Chapel Comprehensive School

CHRISTMAS

C hristmas is a time to celebrate Christ's birth,
H e's coming with His gift to Earth,
R iding high on the crest of a cloud,
I n come the reindeer, pulling the sleigh,
S anta's coming to give us gifts,
T oys all around for the kids,
M um's cooking dinner for the family,
A time for presents to be given out,
S anta's gone for the year, it doesn't matter,
New Year's here.

John Patrick (12)
Holmes Chapel Comprehensive School

The Roller Coaster

R eady to drop
O nly a few more seconds
L owered
L ightning speed
E veryone screaming
R ails clinking

C olours flashing
O ut of the blue
A stonishing bends
S peed dropping
T ime for the last dip
E veryone OK
R elax, it's over!

Dominic Durham (11)
Holmes Chapel Comprehensive School

Friendship

F is for friends.
R is for respect each other.
I is for interesting to know
E is for enthusiastic about things
N is for never letting you down
D is for doing things together
S is for keeping secrets
H is for happy
I is for interested in you
P is for presents you buy each other.

Rebecca Atherton (11)
Holmes Chapel Comprehensive School

SORRY I'M LATE . . .

'Sorry I'm late, Miss,
My hamster ate my homework.'

'Sorry I'm late, Miss,
My hamster just died.'

'Sorry I'm late, Miss,
My shoes ran away.'

'Sorry I'm late, Miss,
I had to see the Queen.'

'Sorry I'm late, Miss,
Aliens abducted me
And made me run 50 laps
'When I got back I found myself in the toilet.'

'Sorry I'm late, Miss,
I could not be bothered to come!'

Eloise Halling (12)
Holmes Chapel Comprehensive School

I WOULD LOVE A PONY!

I would love a pony,
But maybe it would get lonely,
I'd ride him or her every day,
Hopefully along a bay,
I wouldn't complain about getting up early,
Even though my brain goes whirly,
My stable would be top of the lot,
Even a baby would stir in their cot,
I would send it on holiday to Tony's,
I would really love a pony!

Katy Cooper (12)
Holmes Chapel Comprehensive School

The Ride

We were on the funfair ride
Where I pretended there was a tide.

It turned left and right,
My friends were already white.

I was trying not to dream
While my friends let out a scream.

It went even quicker,
So it seemed like a flicker.

It came to a curl
When my mates ended in a twirl.

The ride had come to an end.

Simon Wu (11)
Holmes Chapel Comprehensive School

Hallowe'en!

Hallowe'en, spiders, witches too
Anything spooky or scary will do.
Pumpkins in the windows
Gleaming in the light.

Sweets and chocolate
Any child's delight.

Ghosts in the darkness
Fading away
Sure they'll come back
Another day.

Danielle Coles (12)
Holmes Chapel Comprehensive School

A Jar Of Life

I will put in my jar,
the love from my heart,
the hope given to me by my mum
and the wish of a shooting star.

I will put in my jar,
fun from the Tiny Tods and the laughter
of the friends I play with,
and growth that happens all day and night.

I will put in my jar
regret, what I didn't do, and beauty,
the world is beautiful and so are you.

I will put in my jar,
the hope that made me cry,
the love that broke my heart
and the death that cast over me
and everyone that lived.

Tristan Fellows (11)
Holmes Chapel Comprehensive School

My Roller Coaster Ride

As I reached the top
I heard the clicking
There it was, the big drop
I felt my heart ticking
As it did the loop
I tasted yesterday's soup!

Mitchell Lawrence (12)
Holmes Chapel Comprehensive School

CHRISTMAS DAY

In the night's sky stars shine brightly
And the stars are like sparkling Christmas lights.
Crunchy Christmas cake comes at Christmas dinner,
And Christmas dinner is like a feast of all feasts.
For this is Christmas Day.

Playing with presents, perfects your happiness
And presents make you feel as if you are the king of the world.
My family is either friendly or funny
And family is as important as Tony Blair,
For today is Christmas Day.

Soft, white snow makes you sleep soundly
And snow is like a cold, white blanket.
Fabulous Father Christmas forbids disobedience,
And Father Christmas is like a loving parent to us all.
For today is Christmas Day.

Michael Turner (12)
Holmes Chapel Comprehensive School

THE WIND

The wind is a rush of anger,
With a crack
And a snap,
A tree trunk goes smack
The wind is a rush of anger.

The wind is a rush of anger,
Tearing off rooftops,
Demolishing cities,
Wrenching up crops,
The wind is a rush of anger.

Scott Penlington (11)
Holmes Chapel Comprehensive School

STREETS

People bustling
Bags laden
Ice cream van ringing
Merry-go-round turning
Children laughing
Cars beeping
Lights changing
Babies crying
All in the daytime street.

Lights flicking
Cars screeching
Empty pavements
Eyes gleaming
Doors silent
People huddled
Smoke pluming
Dawn coming
All in the night-time street.

Rebekah Ashmore (11)
Holmes Chapel Comprehensive School

CAMELOT

C ome to Camelot
A nd have a great time
M ake your dreams come true
E njoy your birthday at Camelot
L ots of fun
O pen the magic door
T hen shut it.

Ben Williams (12)
Holmes Chapel Comprehensive School

WAR!

Planes are crashing.
People are dying.
What a place to live!

Not a moment of silence
While guns are firing rapidly.
What a place to live!

Everyone's hiding in their home,
While boats and submarines lie low.
What a place to live!

Now they're bombing Israel
What a terrible thing to do.
Not a single flower left in a field,
'Oh, what a place to live!'

Ben Whittaker (12)
Holmes Chapel Comprehensive School

THE ROLLER COASTER

The clinking and clanking
when we're going up,
all the people going to watch us,
the massive drop in front of us,
scared out of my pants,
hearing screams,
'Ahhhh!' Down we go,
eyes closed,
Nooooo!
Finished at last.

Jonathan Turner (11)
Holmes Chapel Comprehensive School

A Warm Christmas Eve

The fire was burning hot
flaming many colours
yellow, orange, red.
Bright twinkling lights
scattered on the tree
tinsel and toys on branches
filled with Christmas joy.
Nice exotically wrapped presents
all colours and shapes
piled underneath
the green fern tree.
Loud singing is heard all night
carol singers it must be
singing 'La la la' all in a chorus.
Layers of white, cold snow
are falling fast outside
covering people's roofs, gardens and houses.
Excitement is made inside the house
happiness, joy and smiling

because . . . tomorrow is *Christmas Day!*

Ruth Wardley (11)
Holmes Chapel Comprehensive School

The Roller Coaster

As the old cart slowly climbed
The steep and rickety structure
You could hear the clicking stop from behind
The train almost came to a standstill
Growing into a deadly decline.

Joseph Heath (12)
Holmes Chapel Comprehensive School

Writing Poems

Writing poems is so borin'
It simply leaves me snorin'

I can't be bothered to finish the poem
So see you tomorrow, I'm goin'

But just before I go
Think you'd like to know

I am the world's worst poet
And you lot, you all know it

And don't forget writing poems is so borin'
I wouldn't write one else you'll be snorin'

But if like me you've got to write one
Then take my tip and write it on

How boring writing poems is!

Tom Leech (12)
Holmes Chapel Comprehensive School

Tennis

Tennis players swooping
around the tennis court.

Clashing and smashing whatever
the people thought.

Summertime again,
it will never rain.

Moving and accusing it will
never be the same.

Vicky Holt (11)
Holmes Chapel Comprehensive School

School

Oh no, it's time for school
First, it's PE
Got to save the penalty.
Now it's drama.
Got to act well.
Great, it's break.
Time to play with friends.
Then it's tech.
Got to make a moist detector.
Yes, it's lunch.
Time to munch and munch.
Now it's art,
It's so boring.
Last it's English.
Need to write a poem,
Oh yes, it's home time.

Daniel Coppock (12)
Holmes Chapel Comprehensive School

Water

Water
Rushes, gushes,
Swirls, whirls round and round,
Bashes, crashes
Into rocks,
Bubbles into white foam,
Near the edge,
On the edge,
Falls, falls
Down the waterfall.

Charlotte Cawood (11)
Holmes Chapel Comprehensive School

FRIENDS

A lot of people will walk through your life,
But only friends will leave footprints.
Friends are the family you choose for yourself,
Like an eye choosing a target.
They can make you cry with laughter,
Or cry yourself to sleep.
They're the ones who always win,
When everybody else fails.
They're the ones who stick with you,
In your ups and through your downs.
At times you will break up,
But whatever the reason you will make up.
Some friends will come and go,
But true friends will grow and grow.
A lot of people will walk through your life,
But only friends will leave footprints.

Melanie Bott (12)
Holmes Chapel Comprehensive School

MEL

Mel is my best friend,
Our friendship will never end.
She cares for me when I'm feeling down,
We always go shopping in the local town.
We sit together and talk all day,
She understands me and listens to what I say.
We'll always be friends no matter what,
We'll stay together because I like her a lot!

Hannah Gosset (11)
Holmes Chapel Comprehensive School

Getting Ready To Win

The feel of my beautiful pony's muzzle sniffing my hand
As I plait its clean, shiny mane with white and cream bands
Brushing down its warm, lovely coat
The dip in its back like a little rowing boat
Licking the sugar off my hand with its pink tongue
Four taps on the ground with its hooves as we stride along
In the horsebox and we are off to the show
Fingers crossed, hoping to win, looking down at my toes
We are there and getting ready
As we walk over, nerves steady
We are ready to go into the jumping ring
Over the jump as fast as a bird's wing
I have won a rosette, I was better than the rest
My pony is the best!

Caroline Bateman (11)
Holmes Chapel Comprehensive School

Why I Am Late For School

'Sorry, I am late, Sir, but my dog ate my shoes.'
'Sorry I am late, Sir, but I was trampled on by buffaloes
and they came in twos.'
'Sorry I am late, Sir, but I was attacked by dogs that were as dark
as dust in the dark.'
'Sorry, I am late, Sir, but I tripped over a red rock that was rock hard.'
'Sorry I am late, Sir, but I was abducted by aliens as tall as trees.'
'Sorry I am late, Sir, but I fell in a puddle as wet as the sea.'
'Sorry, I am late, Sir, but I was constipated and had to be sedated.'
'Sorry, I was late, Sir, I just didn't want to come.'

Cally Chappelow (12)
Holmes Chapel Comprehensive School

The Wind

The wind howls through the tree branches,
like a wolf hunting down its prey.
The snow falls, fluttering softly, gently, delicately,
then when it touches the ground, it disappears
like it was never there.

In the distance a little cabin waits,
smoke coming from its bellowing chimney,
laughing coming from inside of it.

The wind howls through the mountains,
through the caves and across the plains of ice.
Glaciers cruise down the mountainsides,
shaving away layers of rock until they come to
a slow halt.

Wind, wind, everywhere, up in the sky,
through the clouds, along the ground and over the seas.

Wind, wind, everywhere.

Lewis Bertoni (12)
Holmes Chapel Comprehensive School

The Roller Coaster Ride

Round and round, hanging upside down,
waiting to fall and crash to the ground,
spinning and spinning, lurching and clunking,
the crowds hum like bees below,
the screams of the people in front can be heard,
as they're whirled round and round,
a tunnel's ahead, there's the screeching of brakes
and then, *silence . . .*

Amy Hudson (11)
Holmes Chapel Comprehensive School

Christmas Morning

So excited, just can't sleep,
has he been yet?
Dare I peep?
Sneaking across the landing
down the stairs
and through the hall
then I see all the presents,
tightly wrapped just for me
under the tree,
then a voice yells,
'Back to bed!'

Now it's morning
that's just great,
now I can see the presents properly
there I see, under the tree,
presents just for me,
'Yippee,' I shout,
'That's for me!'

Nick Barlow (12)
Holmes Chapel Comprehensive School

The Roller Coaster Ride

My cart went slowly up the slope,
clink, clink, clink.
Then down went my cart,
whoosh, whoosh!
I heard people screaming,
'Ahh, ahh, ahhh!'
I wanted to go again,
and again and again!

Simon Pilkington (11)
Holmes Chapel Comprehensive School

HAIKUS FOR SEASONS!

Spring brings little lambs,
Hopping around in the fields,
With a hop, skip, jump!

Summer's baby birds,
Whistle in the treetops high,
Flapping fluffy wings!

Autumn's leaves turn brown,
Camouflaging red squirrels,
Scrabbling on the ground!

Winter has white snow,
Like a magical kingdom,
Crispy under feet!

These cheerful seasons,
Very different times of year,
I would keep all four!

Gemma Styles (11)
Holmes Chapel Comprehensive School

THE MEMORISING COMPUTER

The memorising computer
Searching the infinite Internet
Clever, entertaining, experienced
Like an unfound brainbox
Like a high-speed motor machine
It makes me feel incredibly lazy
Like a child hiding at the back of the class
The memorising computer
Reminds us of the latest technology.

Oliver Jones (11)
Holmes Chapel Comprehensive School

BONFIRE NIGHT

The hedgehog retreats,
Dogs bark,
Cats run to the house,
It's come once again.

Crackle, flicker, roar,
The greedy monster leaps up,
'Ooh!' 'Aah!'
The crowd shouts.

At this time,
The sky is lit up,
Its colours are bright,
Blue, red, pink, gold.

Bonfire Night!
The Catherine wheel spits,
Fireworks bang,
Fountains flicker.

Rosy red faces,
Look on in earnest,
Their sparklers sparkle,
Making lines in the night sky.

When all the fireworks are used,
People start to go
Their separate ways,
It will come again next year.

The hedgehog snuffles,
Dogs run around,
Cats climb trees,
It's been once again.

Natalie Davenport (12)
Holmes Chapel Comprehensive School

THE COASTER

I came up to the top
In my carriage
very scared
halt!
We came
to a standstill
I waited
watching
the dots
below.
Then
it happened!
Whoosh!
We
plunged down
    a
      a
        a
          a
            h!
My stomach
came up
into my throat
my tummy was
turning
round
and
round!
Over!
What a relief!

Aaron Francis Collis (11)
Holmes Chapel Comprehensive School

THE ROLLER COASTER

The steel mountain creaks and groans,
The carriages climb its rusted path,
It reaches the peak, the structure moans,
There is silence, then a nervous laugh,
Then it

p
l
u
m
m
e
t
s

d
o
w
n!

Bradley M Wilson (12)
Holmes Chapel Comprehensive School

NEMESIS

My hands were shaking
We started to go, *whoosh!*
I started to scream
Closed my eyes
I opened them again
I was upside down
Not near the ground
Aarrgghh!

Mia Wellavize (12)
Holmes Chapel Comprehensive School

The Football

I used to belong to a baby,
Who dribbled all over my skin,
But then he got a bit older
And kicked me in the bin.

A truck came around in the morning
And I was put into it,
A young teenager found me
And said that I would fit.

There was a match that Saturday,
Which gave me a great big scare,
We lost, I got thrown away,
I'll never fit in, it's not fair.

Douglas Corbishley (11)
Holmes Chapel Comprehensive School

Where Do All The Teachers Go?

Where do all the teachers go
When it's 4 o'clock?
Do they live in houses
And do they wash their socks?

Do they wear pyjamas?
And do they watch TV?
And do they pick their noses
The same as you and me?

I'll follow one back home today
I'll find out what they do
Then I'll put it in a poem
That they can read to you!

Stephanie Brook (11)
Holmes Chapel Comprehensive School

My Autumn Window

I look out of my window
I see the golden brown leaves scattered
All over the floor
The trees swaying their empty branches
The sky, the dull sky
It's cold today.

I look out of my window
I see the night sky
I can just make out the clouds
I see the outline of the trees still swaying.
Silent. It's silent.

I look out of my window
I see the geese flying south
I hear the cold birds singing
It's still dull.
The branches still empty.
The golden leaves still scattered
All over the floor.
No change.
One change -
It's snowing.

I look out of my window
I see the dull sky falling white
I see the empty branches covered in snow
The grass safe under its wintry blanket
I hear the geese flying south
I hear the cold birds singing
I feel the cold.

It's all in my autumn window.

Alice Tate (11)
Holmes Chapel Comprehensive School

A Locket Of Love

I will put in my locket

The word 'love' in all the languages
The peace of a united world
The first kiss of a married couple

I will put in my locket

A witch with a wand
A fairy with a cauldron
And the smell of a welcoming barbecue

I will put in my locket

Snow from the summit of Mount Everest
A drop of water from the deepest well
And a ball of fire from the centre of the Earth

I will put in my locket

The first light in a baby's eye
The last breath of an ancient king
And a slide along a rainbow leading to Heaven.

My locket is fashioned of silver bark
From a weeping willow,
Its hinges are the horn of a unicorn
And its fastening; crystal of an underground cavern.

I will bury my locket
At the bottom of the deepest ocean,
So when it seems the Earth is coming to its end
I can open the locket and the world will be filled with love
once again.

Sarah Hopwood (12)
Holmes Chapel Comprehensive School

The Evils Of Darkness

A great beast is an ogre,
With spiky club and more,
A great beast is an ogre,
With helmet, tooth and claw,
A great beast is an ogre,
A giant among men,
A great beast is an ogre,
As strong as at least ten.

A weak beast is a goblin,
Stealing from the fallen,
A weak beast is a goblin,
Running if they call him,
A weak beast is a goblin,
Running from the battle,
A weak beast is a goblin,
Weaker than a rattle.

A stupid beast a troll is,
Lumbering towards me,
A stupid beast a troll is,
Hoping to destroy me.
A stupid beast a troll is,
With loincloth and with bone,
A stupid beast a troll is,
For he is made from stone.

Andrew Roberts (12)
Holmes Chapel Comprehensive School

The 20p Strawberry Bonbon

A 20p strawberry bonbon,
It tastes great, yet it causes fights every day.
Only last week, 6 men fought for 6 days
On a 6 storey building in Ipswich.

They each claimed they loved the taste
More than the others . . .
It ended tragically, as all but one was bloody and injured,
All over a 20p strawberry bonbon.

Jack Carr (11)
Holmes Chapel Comprehensive School

The Ticket That Changed A Sad Life

This is a poem about a boy,
In his short life he had no joy.
His mum and dad had no jobs,
They were even known as the slobs.

Because of this they had no money,
Children at school found this funny.
They laughed at him and made him cry,
The little boy didn't understand why.

One day his mum found a pound,
It was just lying upon the ground.
With the pound she bought a ticket,
The little boy helped her pick it.

That night the family watched the draw,
They couldn't believe what they saw.
Up came the numbers they had chosen,
The family sat as if they'd frozen.

At last the boy learned how to live his life,
The children at school gave him no more strife.
The little boy learned how to smile,
He no longer felt like he was on trial.

Ben Barron (12)
Holmes Chapel Comprehensive School

The River

The river is a child, a youth, a juvenile,
A river on a long journey, a trip, a route
Crawling along as toddlers do
Singing a song out of tune.

The river's getting rougher now, gruff, hoarse
The river's getting faster now, speedy, quick,
Jumping gracefully over rocks.

The river's getting older now, aged and elderly
Ready to stop, break off and close
Into the sea it goes
And now is part of a bigger family.

Rochelle Christian (11)
Holmes Chapel Comprehensive School

Poems Are Really Boring To Write!

Poems are really boring to write,
It's more fun to fly a kite,
It's like watching paint dry
And you know I'd just rather die!

Poems are really boring to read,
They're usually as long as my dog's lead,
It's like reading a whole book,
I'd rather be a thieving crook!

But there is something I want to ask,
Do you like my poem?

Georgina Brider (12)
Holmes Chapel Comprehensive School

ON A DARK STORMY NIGHT

A dark stormy night is:
When mummies and skeletons roam the night,
When evil is out and about,
When children sleep and monsters eat
And unexpecting children sleep,
When evil roams the night,
When giants come out to feast,

And the night is black as monsters,
And the moon is full and bright,

And the night is ruled by monsters,
And the night is ruled by monsters.

And then suddenly, out comes the morning light;
Bright comes the sun, shining bright,
And the monster's reign is over
Until night comes again. Until night comes again.

James Lowrie (12)
Holmes Chapel Comprehensive School

WAITING TO BEGIN

Their soft velvety nose twitches with excitement,
Their eyes twinkle in the soft light,
Their ears pricked hearing the commentator,
Their long mane plaited to show their smooth neck,
Their slimline legs stamp with eagerness,
Their tail swishes in the roar of the crowd,
Their body relaxed but eager to win.

Penny Hancox (12)
Holmes Chapel Comprehensive School

THE CHEST OF FANTASY!

I will put in the chest

The last golden ray of sunlight on a summer evening
A slice of a rainbow over a green valley
A hair from the tail of a golden unicorn

I will put in the chest

A bolt of lightning crashing down from a purple cloudy sky
The smell of a sweet black rose on a bitter winter day
A glittering star falling from the dark sky scattering light across
an icy land

I will put in the chest

A swirl of sand from a vast and deserted desert baking in the sun
The love of a mother for her newborn child
A wisp of smoke from the belly of an ancient dragon

I will put in the chest

The first laugh of a baby transforming into a thousand fairies
glittering in the moonlight
A bright yellow daffodil growing up from a frosting of winter snow
on a cold November day
The last words of a great king, heard by the world at the end of an era.

The chest is carved from the wings of angels and coated in magic dust
Its hinges are fashioned from ice glaciers deep down in the earth
Its core is a piece of wood from the oldest tree on Earth
And inside it's lined with wool from a baby lamb

I will travel on my chest to the top of the highest mountain and the bottom of the deepest valley
I will rediscover Atlantis and walk through the streets again,
go back to the dinosaurs and see the woolly mammoth
Travel to the centre of the Earth and to the end of the universe
I will relive the stories in my books and make the characters come alive.

Catherine Gome (12)
Holmes Chapel Comprehensive School

Baby Boy

'Well done,' said the nurse, 'it's a beautiful baby boy.'
'Thank you,' I replied, 'we've decided to call him Troy.'
She said, 'You'll be able to take him home, in just a day or two.
Keep him wrapped up warm or he could catch a dose of flu.'
Then she handed him over - I stroked his tiny feet.
The next day Daddy came to take us home.
Just as we walked in, I heard the ringing of the phone.
It was Troy's Auntie Judith to offer her congrats.
'I hope he won't grow up to be like my two little brats!
You'll never guess what they did today.
They blocked up the bath with modelling clay.'
There were many more phone calls following on from that.
Each time for more than 20 minutes I was sat.
Eventually I could take no more and took it off the hook.
Then gladly headed off to bed with Troy and a baby book.

Alex Hubbard (11)
Holmes Chapel Comprehensive School

Roller Coaster

Bursting with anticipation
Harnessed securely
Waiting . . .
Waiting . . .
Murmuring machine
Then . . .
Jerk!
The ride begins
I see
The tangled track awaiting me
Buzzing with fear
Cranking and clinking
Ascending the steel serpent
Reaching the peak
Reluctance holds me back
Anticipation pushing me on
Holding my breath
Scared to open my eyes . . .
But past the point of no return:
Then . . . *whoosh!*
Descending rapidly
Cascading and whirring down the structure
Exploding with exhilaration
Hurricane force winds
Whistling and screeching
Tearing at my face
Involuntary screaming
Too soon, slowing down
Relish the experience
Wanting to repeat.

Cathy Spence (11)
Holmes Chapel Comprehensive School

CAUTION

(The following poem is not suitable for mature readers!)

Knock, knock!
    Who's there?
Myself!
    Yourself who?
That's right
    You who!
That's what I want to know!
What's what you want to know?
    You who!
Yes, you've got it!
    You're right!
What's right?
    Yes, I have a whatsright on a chain!
    Yes!
Yes what?
    What's right!
That's what I want to know!
What's what you want to know?
I told you!
I'm not telling you again!
But, what's right?
Y e e e e e s s s s s!
Yes what? Yes, it's with me

Where are you?

        Knock, knock!

            Go away now!

Alexander Moss (11)
Holmes Chapel Comprehensive School

CHRISTMAS EVE

Hooray, it's Christmas tomorrow
Christmas is nearly here
We've put the Christmas tree up
My stocking is hung above the fire
I've left Santa his mince pie and for
Rudolph, I've left him a carrot.

Hooray, it's Christmas tomorrow
Christmas is nearly here
I'm off carol singing now
Whilst Mum cooks the turkey in the oven
And Dad puts the lights up on the house.

Hooray, it's Christmas tomorrow
Christmas is nearly here
I've had a bath, I've brushed my teeth
All I need to do is go to bed
But wait, I need to write my Christmas list
to Santa.

Hooray, it's Christmas tomorrow
Christmas is nearly here.
I'm finally going to bed
Everything is ready at last
And I really can't wait for tomorrow.

Kathryn Atherton (11)
Holmes Chapel Comprehensive School

FRIENDSHIP

If you trust a friend
Your friend will trust you.
Keep their secrets,
They will keep yours,
That's how friends work!

Be happy with them,
They will repay you.
Stick up for them,
They will give you it back,
That's how friends work!

Hannah Barker (11)
Holmes Chapel Comprehensive School

SCHOOL

'My paper's ripped in half, Miss,
My writing's gone all funny.
My cold is coming back, Miss,
My nose is going runny.'

'My eyes are going blurry, Miss,
The book has fallen apart.
Can we do some drama, Miss?
Will I get a part?'

'I don't understand my homework, Sir,
The graphs are going weird.
My pen's run out of ink, Sir
And my pencil's gone all queer!'

'I didn't forget my homework, Miss,
The dog ate it up.
It isn't a classic excuse, Miss,
He's only a little pup.'

'My school bag's strap's come off, Miss.
The books are across town.
What are you going to do to me, Miss?
You're going to make me drown!'

Jenny Hall (12)
Holmes Chapel Comprehensive School

ROLLER COASTER RIDE

I climb into the seat
Hold on tight with my hands and feet

Here we go
Nice and slow
It takes a while
But still I smile
Butterflies in my tummy
It feels really funny
Up it climbs to the top
And quickly I stop
Here we go
Now not slow!
Falling from the sky
I can fly!
At the speed of sound
Down to the ground
Up in the air
Wind in my hair
What a great height
My face turns white
Back down to land
Sweat on my hand
As it goes quicker
I feel sicker
I yell and scream
It's like a bad dream
This is not fun
I want my mum!
One last dip
Tighter I grip
Now going slow
Tears start to flow

At last I am still
I feel ever so ill

Out I get
Face all wet

An ache in my belly
My legs are like jelly

What a nightmare ride
Thought I had died.

Never, never *again!*
Down here I'll remain!

Adam Bautista-Harvey (12)
Holmes Chapel Comprehensive School

THE COLD SEA

(This poem is about a boy named Michael and his great adventure in the sea and it was a book called 'Kensuke's Kingdom' that inspired me to write it)

Michael regretted not putting his lifejacket on,
He was cold in the sea as the moon shone.
Michael was sleepy and all,
Whilst he was clinging onto his football.
Michael was slowly dying,
Shouting, singing and crying.
Hc had no hopc,
No luck, couldn't cope.
Michael's head was getting numb,
After he wished that he'd never come . . .

Anthony Johnston (11)
Holmes Chapel Comprehensive School

My Dog

A tiny puppy,
Silky, snuffly.

Scampering around
Loud and proud.

Cute and cuddly,
Always getting muddy.

Getting bigger,
Little tiger.

Gorgeous, lovely,
That's my puppy.

From a tiny puppy
To a giant dog.

I love my dog!

Paige Stokes (11)
Holmes Chapel Comprehensive School

The Beast

Fiery breath
Smelling like death
Most blood-red
Like the dead
Olive green
Really mean
We are a feast
To the beast
But after eating all
He is still small.

Rebecca Smith (12)
Holmes Chapel Comprehensive School

Bonfire Night

Fireworks shine,
Sparklers glow,
Bonfires crackle,
People say, 'Woah!'

Up with a bang,
See colours shine,
Come outside,
It's firework time.

Cheerful people
Eat their food,
Smiling, happy
In a good mood.

It only happens
Once a year,
So let's go out
And make a cheer!

Caroline Tarrant (12)
Holmes Chapel Comprehensive School

What Am I?

My tummy is big
My tail is long
I jump up and down
All day long.

I live where it's hot
And that's my lot.

What am I?
Answer - A kangaroo!

Jess Gosling (12)
Holmes Chapel Comprehensive School

Flakes Of Snow

They fall so high, in the glistening sky
And yet nothing can compete
When the crystals float and sway.

They twist and they turn,
Their delicate patterns
Are all so different,
There is never one the same.

Unique is how I describe them,
They're as precious as roses,
They are trinkets of beauty.

Sadly they come to their end
And melt so suddenly.
They only last a minute or two
But they hold frozen loveliness.

Emily Lonsdale (12)
Holmes Chapel Comprehensive School

Rugby

I love rugby
The bellowing of the players
The scrums, the rucks, the mauls
Being in a rugby game is like
Being in a thunderstorm,
Crashing all around you.
Passing the ball before getting tackled
Try-scoring wingers fast like the wind
I love rugby.

James Mitchell (11)
Holmes Chapel Comprehensive School

When I Was Born

When I was born
My mother said I looked like an Easter egg
With chocolate poured over me.
When I was born
My father said I was a trick on Hallowe'en
Wearing a vampire mask.
When I was born
My sister said I was a Christmas present,
They opened me up and saw something good.
When I was born
My granny said
I was a harvest gift,
Given to the needy.
When I was born
I think I was me.

Matthew Smith (12)
Holmes Chapel Comprehensive School

Hippies

There was an old hippie called Gypsy Rose,
She had a really big nose,
She lived in a VW camper for a house,
She had lots of crystals and a big mouse,
Her clothes were really out-of-date,
And she had a pretty daughter called Kate,
She had dark brown and pink hair
And she didn't really care.
She went to Woodstock and her camper van
wouldn't stop.
She went through the crowds and everyone shouted,
'Peace' out loud!

Sarah Gardiner (11)
Holmes Chapel Comprehensive School

Guess Who?

If my person was a colour, they would be gold and white.
If my person was a season, they would be autumn,
You can't guess what colour the leaves would turn.
If my person was a place, they would be England.
If my person was a weather, they would be storms and
the beautiful sunrise.
If my person was an item of clothing, they would be a ballgown
with jewels and diamonds.
If my person was furniture, they would be a mirror, engraved
with crowns.
If my person was a TV show, they would be a history documentary.
If my person was a food, they would be a beautiful gateaux, perfect
in every way.

Can you guess who my person is?

Queen Elizabeth I

Rebecca Steer (12)
Holmes Chapel Comprehensive School

Saffy's Angel

The dream is a distant memory.
She's in the beautiful garden, holding onto her angel, crying.
She leaves it behind in Siena, and travels to a place unknown.
Years later she finds a note and the search for her angel begins.
She stows away to Siena to try and find her past.
Days later she's back in the garden.
She searches high and low, but she cannot find her angel.
She travels back home to her family, where a surprise is waiting for her.
'Saffy, Saffy, we've found your angel.'
Then Saffy felt like she belonged.

Holly Mitchell (12)
Holmes Chapel Comprehensive School

THE POT OF POISON AND FEAR

I will put in my pot
The oldest snake from a cave underground,
The deadliest poison from a night-black scorpion,
The worst smell from a rotting skunk.

I will put in my pot
The first dead tree from the garden of death,
A last scream from a dying enemy,
A cure to all hope and happiness.

I will put in my pot
The dagger of all deathly dreams,
The sound of a rifle splitting the sky,
The sad cry of a much loved mother.

I will put in my pot
A builder with a gun,
A thief with a hammer,
The screech of a strangled cat.

My pot is styled from
The deadliest venom from a newborn snake,
The hinges are the thumb joints of the oldest woman
And the lid is a yellow toenail from a baby giant's toe.

Jemima Jo Lloyd (12)
Holmes Chapel Comprehensive School

ROLLER COASTER

I felt the pit in my stomach as it reached the summit.
My fear climbed as the carriage lurched.
Adrenalin rushed as the mighty carriage plunged,
Like a dragon swooping.

Sarah Forrester (12)
Holmes Chapel Comprehensive School

Falling Asleep

I feel very sleepy as I clamber into bed.
I smell the fresh cornfield swaying in the quiet breeze.
I hear the cars as they drive past my window.
I see the trees casting shadows on the road.

I hear the television on downstairs.
I see the light slowly fading in the hall.
I smell the sweet candles on my window sill.
I feel the warmth of my bed.

I hear the beat of my own heart.
I feel myself sink into my pillow.
I smell the night's air for the last time.
I see the first glimpse of a dream.

Elizabeth Jenkins (12)
Holmes Chapel Comprehensive School

Hope

Hope is a beautiful butterfly
Fluttering in the warm summer breeze,
A delicate yellow daffodil
Swaying gently in the sun.
Hope is an amazing blue lake glimmering,
A baby duckling all soft and downy.
Hope is a white cloud floating high up in the sky,
A strawberry mousse on your tongue
On a hot summer's day.
Hope is your family and friends,
A great big hug from the one you love.

Kate Mills (12)
Holmes Chapel Comprehensive School

The Magic Bottle

I would put in my bottle
A golden phoenix that I would ride every day,
A magic genie for lots of wishes,
The best theme park in the world.

I would put in my bottle
The sweetest tasting cake that anyone ever baked,
A credit card that never runs out,
A sweet shop that keeps on rolling.

I would put in my bottle
A serum that would grant immortality,
A part of cloud 9,
A pot of gold from the end of a rainbow.

Matthew Wake (12)
Holmes Chapel Comprehensive School

January Winds And Gales

January, January,
On a winter's night
The wind is gushing
And the birds are tumbling.
On a dark, cold night
As I cuddlc up to my duvct
I hear my baby sister screaming for help.
Then I hear some footsteps on the shallow, creaky floorboards,
I can't get to sleep because I can hear my wind chime
Clanging on my door.
All of a sudden it's peaceful and quiet,
At last it's calm, so now it's time for us to sleep.

Danniella Joslin (11)
Holmes Chapel Comprehensive School

A SHOOTING STAR

A shooting star darts and dashes
And dives in all directions,
It swirls and twirls
And whips and whirls
And shows off when it dances.

A shooting star brightens up the sky,
Shines as bright as sunlight,
Its little tail flickers from side to side
To gain up all its speed,
All to brighten up the sky.

But when night fades away
And morning dawns,
The shooting star becomes -
Still and dreamy.

Helen Coghlan (11)
Holmes Chapel Comprehensive School

MY BUNNIES

The bunnies that hop around
Intrude on other grounds.
Their ears are big and fluffy,
They have dirt digging claws,
A pink scruffy nose,
Nice tapping feet.
The other scruffy bunnies
Are so funny,
That's why they're my bunnies.

Vicki Hunt (11)
Holmes Chapel Comprehensive School

A Losing Battle

Walk through the forest,
Birds are flying by,
Walking through a field,
Sheep are nearby,
Walking along a stream,
Fish are swimming by.

Look-out,
Off a hill,
Nature's at high,
Turn around,
Disaster!
Factories taking over,
Land in short supply,
Nature won't give up now,
Try to keep its ground,
There's no way to save itself.

Nature will die.

George McDowell (11)
Holmes Chapel Comprehensive School

Roller Coaster Ride

I get onto the monster
Hearing electricity buzzing
And we're off
Whizzing through the air
Then plummeting down
Around the bend
Up the tracks, and down again
And then . . . nothing!

Alison Cartwright (12)
Holmes Chapel Comprehensive School

Train

It comes so fast
Like the speed of light,
Like a bullet with an extra blast,
Get in its way and you'll get a fright.

Horn so loud it could be heard
All around the world.
The train comes past,
Its sound a blast
And makes the bird's wing unfold.

The track so shiny for its wheels to rest on,
The lights will shine upon the bridge
Which from far away looks so midge.

As soon as you step in you're at risk,
Your heart, any time, could stop like a dish.
Lots of years still for your life,
Train will crash and you feel like you've
been stabbed by a knife.

Scott Barker (11)
Holmes Chapel Comprehensive School

No Meaning

No words would come before these,
And now they drift with such ease.
This poem has no meaning nor a theme,
Like a fantasy, like a dream.
No words are sailing through my head
But flow onto the paper instead.

Rochelle Silverstein (11)
Holmes Chapel Comprehensive School

MY SAFE OF WISHES

I will put in my safe
The feather of a phoenix,
The last surviving dinosaur,
A great big theme park.

I will put in my safe
A skate park for everyone in Holmes Chapel
Because no one else will build one for us,
A drink of golden water for eternal life and youth,
The ability to fly,
A wad of money
For everyone in poorer countries.

I will put in my safe
A solution to world peace,
A happy world for lucky people
And a world without things that hurt.
My box is made of gold and silver
And spikes all over it to stop it getting into the wrong hands
And I will hold the only key.

James Miller (12)
Holmes Chapel Comprehensive School

SPORTS

He is as red as a Man United T-shirt.
He's warm like a casual man.
He's a summer person that does Sports Daily.
If he was a piece of clothing he would be a pair of sweaty pants.
He's a medal that he is proud of!

David Beckham

Jack Willsdon (11)
Holmes Chapel Comprehensive School

A Cat Called Whiskey

There was a cat called Whiskey
Who liked to play very risky.
He had a red button nose
That looked a bit like a rose.
He had little white mittens,
Mind you so did his kittens.

He married a cat called Tigger
Who was a bit of a digger.
They had a kitten called Pinks
Who liked to play tiddlywinks,
For argue they did never,
So happily they lived forever.

Byron Murgatroyd (11)
Holmes Chapel Comprehensive School

The Blank Page

Look at it,
Staring up at me,
A blank page
And I need to fill it,
A whole page,
What can I write? What?
Come on, think,
Only five minutes left,
Got to write,
I have to fill the white.

Hey, look, it's full!

Duncan McKenna (12)
Holmes Chapel Comprehensive School

MY CHEST OF JOY!

In my chest of joy I would put
The most glistening ring in the world,
A drop of water from the freshest waterfall,
The bounciest cloud in the sky.

In my chest of joy I would put
The biggest ray of light,
The prettiest flower ever seen,
The love of God for everybody who asks for it.

In my chest of joy I would put
The most beautiful smile from a baby,
A wish that will come true,
A cure for all deaths.

Hayley Coutts (12)
Holmes Chapel Comprehensive School

HOLE IN THE PAGE

There's a hole in my page,
What shall I do?
I'll stick it together with paper and glue,
But that won't do.

There's a hole in my page,
How shall I fix it?
I'll take it to the doctors
And then they'll fix it,
But that won't do.

There's a hole in my page,
How shall I mend it?

Thomas Beeston (12)
Holmes Chapel Comprehensive School

The Cave Of Death

I will put in my cave

Vultures from a South American desert,
A dagger from the world's most wanted killer,
Poison from the black fountain.

I will put in my cave

Everlasting darkness from a hidden cavern,
From a dark tunnel, dragon's fire,
The last tree cut down.

I will put in my cave

A scream from a frightened child,
A mouldy skeleton from a graveyard,
Stagnant water from a bottomless pit.

I will put in my cave

A meteor about to hit Earth,
An illness with no cure,
A smell to cover the world.

My cave is made of slime,
With doors of smoke
And bones as hinges.

In my cave I will injure animals and humans,
Mix potions
And create havoc worldwide.

Joanna Scott (12)
Holmes Chapel Comprehensive School

My Loved Animals

I love my cat
but she doesn't like my rat
so she stays in her cage
to be safe.

I love my dog
but he chases my hog
and my frog doesn't
like it anyway.

I love my quail
but it pecks at my whale
so he swims to the
bottom of the pool.

I love my kangaroo
but he tries to eat my shrew
so he runs and hides
in the loo.

I love my little pony
but he gets very lonely
so I visit him as often
as I can.

I love my funny parrot
who's partial to a carrot
so I give him one or two
in a stew.

Francesca Fulton (11)
Holmes Chapel Comprehensive School

About Sherbet Lemons

When I saw it, it looked like a little lemon.
The last time I had one, I think I was seven.

For a sherbet lemon, it felt very sticky.
Just like the mushy peas down at the chippy.

I put it in my mouth, oh what a delight!
Sherbet slithered out, nearly before the bite.

Chomp and there it was crushed.
I wish I had saved it, I wish it wasn't mushed.

The teacher collected the wrappers when we all had one each.
But Chris was really hungry and said,
'Miss, can I have another one, please?'

Michael Rhodes (12)
Holmes Chapel Comprehensive School

A Lemon Sherbet

With a whoosh of Lemon Fanta, bubbly and bright,
Smooth, sticky sides and a surprise inside.
Fizzy, squishy and tart, the sherbet explodes
With a mouth-watering delight.
Smaller and smaller it's getting now,
The fizzing has stopped and the lemon has crumbled,
Oh no it's all gone!

Charlotte Sheehan (12)
Holmes Chapel Comprehensive School

My Box Of Hope

I will put in my box of hope

World peace and happiness
And the past so I can go back in time and see Grandad
And two day weeks where Christmas comes soon.

I will put in my box of hope

A fountain of happiness which makes all the sad
And angry people be happy with each other
And a pencil case which is full of glittery pens which never run out
And a locket which holds very happy memories from my past.

I will put in my box of hope

A tree of stars which light up the dark black sky
And a pen which writes out rules of love and kindness
And a book which tells us that we're all special
That's what I put in the box.

Rachael Bond (11)
Holmes Chapel Comprehensive School

Roller Coaster

Click, click, click, silence,
The fear and excitement fight inside me,
I close my eyes and wish I was at home,
My stomach drops,
I'm safe.

Francesca Worthington (12)
Holmes Chapel Comprehensive School

The Vault Of Dreams

I will put in the vault

A healing shadow that heals all wounds,
A small, creamy-white dove holding an eternal declaration of
peace for the world,
An island of tranquillity for people to get away from a stressful life.

I will put in the vault

A bottomless purse for poor and bankrupt families,
A solid house for the homeless to have shelter of their own,
A banquet for millions of famished people to enjoy.

I will put in the vault

The last dinner baked by a caring mum,
The last sports game watched by a busy dad,
The last lie told by a mischievous sister.

Thomas Barr (11)
Holmes Chapel Comprehensive School

Guess Who?

He is red, like a determined bull.
He is winter, as cool as ice when he does what he does.
He is a train station because he's always ready for the next.
He is lightning, as quick as a flash.
He would be a watch, always there when needed.
He would be a hard marble fireplace, nearly impossible to go through.
He would be who he wants to be, a millionaire, taking risks.
He would be fish and chips, typical English.

A: Rio Ferdinand.

Michael Boon (12)
Holmes Chapel Comprehensive School

JORDAN

My person is a strong magenta,
As beautiful as a rose and twice as thorny.

My person is a spring day
With an ice cream giving out cones!

My person is the Alps
High snow-topped peaks.

My person is a thirty-two double E cami top,
Good looking, supportive and cheeky
(Not to mention 50% synthetic fabric).

My person is mistral wind one minute,
Calm then *wham!*

My person would be a BMX with overpumped tyres.

My person is a soap opera, a regular drama.

My person is a cream cake overflowing
And slightly sickening.

James Stanier (12)
Holmes Chapel Comprehensive School

ODE TO A BLADE OF GRASS

Oh to be a piece of grass, it is never known,
People never care how you feel, being mown, being sown.

Trampled on, how do they dare?
On your own, but then again never left alone,
But once you're dead, your baby shall meet the same.

Tom Chambers (11)
Holmes Chapel Comprehensive School

THE FOUNTAIN OF DREAMS

I will put in the fountain
A newborn rabbit sniffing the scents of the world,
The last pink blossom to fall to the ground
And a great white horse with a silvery flowing mane.

I will put in the fountain
A pod of dolphins mirroring each other against the night's sky,
A drop of dew on the green summer's grass
And a fairy astride a flying foal.

I will put in the fountain
A baby's first step as she learns to walk,
An owl's hoot on a winter's night
And a star trying its best to light the night's sky.

I will put in the fountain
The cure for cancer so no one will die of it,
A golden pen that always writes the right answer
And the treasures of the ocean sinking beneath the sand.

Rachel Jackson (11)
Holmes Chapel Comprehensive School

WHITE HORSE, BLACK HORSE

White horse, black horse galloping down a hill,
White horse, black horse, do they ever stand still?
Black horse, white horse chomping tons of grass,
Black horse, white horse, it really takes some class -
To have such a shiny, glossy coat,
They neigh from the back of their long, strong throat,
White horse, black horse galloping down a hill.

Kate Powell (11)
Holmes Chapel Comprehensive School

WINNIE THE POOH

Winnie the Pooh is a golden yellow,
He's soft and cuddly like a marshmallow.

If he were a season, he would be them all
Because I know he wouldn't mind at all.

If he were a place, he would be a pool
Because he's like a big wave coming to rule.

Out of a piece of clothing, he would be a shoe
Because I know he would come with me too.

Out of the weather, he would be a hot sunny day
Because I know he would be fun and come out to play.

If Winnie the Pooh was a piece of furniture, he would be a chair
Because I know I could always find him there.

If he were a TV show, he would be 'The Weakest Link'
Because he would always come off pink.

If Winnie the Pooh was a food, he would be a plate of jelly
Because he would be as wobbly as a fat tubby belly.

That's why I love him so much.

Charlotte Basford (12)
Holmes Chapel Comprehensive School

THE ROLLER COASTER

As you reach the top
You feel a surge of pure fear race through you,
You plummet like you're going down to Hell,
It stops,
It's over.

David Bowman (12)
Holmes Chapel Comprehensive School

The Chest Of Passion

I will put in my chest

A single droplet of the fountain of youth,
The piercing hole of a dragon's tooth,
The elegant neck of a snow-white swam.
The last heart of love when all else has gone.

A soft silk cloud floating along,
The whispering rivers chanting their song,
A sprouting bud getting ready to live,
A good close friend that is willing to give.

A golden unicorn galloping across the sky,
A worn-out old man getting ready to die,
The icy crystals of the caves below,
The firing arrow of a hunter's bow.

The never-ending rings of an old oak tree,
The never-ending rainbow that shines down on me,
The ancient cry of a distant whale,
The unknown story of my childhood tale.

Ben Johnson (11)
Holmes Chapel Comprehensive School

Dolphin

As it swiftly sweeps through the sea,
Eyes as glistening as jewels,
In front of boats it weaves the waves, no rules.
This beautiful creature
Has a lot of fun,
So next time you go swimming
The sea's already spun!

Chloe Burcham (11)
Holmes Chapel Comprehensive School

The Secret Saddlebag Of Hope

I will put in my bag:
A golden bird with rubies for eyes
With a song that can wake the dead,
A magic fox with the speed of light
And the magic of a wizard,
A silver cow with a golden tail
With everlasting milk.

I will put in my bag:
A beautiful Arab stallion with a golden mane and tail,
With the speed of a car and the beauty of a rose,
A glowing Arab herd galloping after their leader
With enough strength to pull a mountain,
A cat that can catch and kill an elephant
To feed the homeless.

I will put in my bag:
A dog who can protect the most precious things,
A sheep who never dies to give away its meat,
It does not feel pain, it doesn't feel heat,
A rocking horse that really moves
To keep the children entertained.

I will put in my bag:
A healing unicorn to heal the sick and weak,
A bright red phoenix with the light
To light the darkest corner,
A tiger to make sure that no one breaks the law
So that peace can stay in a small city.

My secret saddlebag of hope is to help the poor
And fill with all the things inside it
And to make the world a place we want to live in.

Jennifer Wright (11)
Holmes Chapel Comprehensive School

The Bag Of Delights

I shall put in my bag

The best football match in history,
The last shooting star,
All the magic tricks of David Blaine.

I shall put in my bag

The fastest car ever made,
The first pot of gold from the end of a rainbow,
The first crunch of a frosty morn.

I shall put in my bag

A cure for all diseases,
An ending to all wars, for world peace,
The funniest comedian ever heard.

My bag is made up out of cards and stars,
Gold, metal and frost.

This is my bag of delights.

Chris Wood (12)
Holmes Chapel Comprehensive School

Wind

Wind is like a raging rhino
Firing past, like a bullet out of a gun,
Hitting anything in its way.
Wind is like a wandering tortoise,
Drifting slowly through the air,
Gentle and calming as a mum.

Gareth Stevens (11)
Holmes Chapel Comprehensive School

A Magical Poem

Magic potions, magic hats,
Magic frogs and magic cats.
Flying, soaring through the air,
Up and down and in a chair.

Dragons, beasts, monsters too,
Invisible potions and bright green goo!
Rabbits in hats and magic shows,
Kiss a toad, see evil crows.

Leg of toad and hair of dog,
Eye of newt and tusk of hog.
Mix them up, add a lightning strike,
Magic is the stuff I like!

Tom Pullan-Boothroy (11)
Holmes Chapel Comprehensive School

Skateboarders Rule

When you hear rolling what do you think?
I think of skateboarders
Zooming towards me like a chariot of death,
Rampaging at you like a bullet.
They don't see you while aimlessly daydreaming
And you are in the middle of the path.
Wood and flesh collide,
You feel pain!
Pain into the side like a sharp dart.
Climbing to your feet you scan the area,
But he is nowhere to be seen.
Once found you ask him,
'Can you teach me that?'

Robbie Cullen (11)
Holmes Chapel Comprehensive School

POWERFUL PLANETS!

Neptune, Neptune,
A cold, gas planet.
Neptune, Neptune,
It can't be that cool . . . can it?

Mercury, Mercury,
A planet of our galaxy.
Mercury, Mercury,
Everyone likes it . . . or is it just me?

Venus, Venus,
Way up in the skies.
Venus, Venus,
Really nice . . . or is it just my eyes?

Pluto, Pluto,
Known as Planet X.
Pluto, Pluto
Whatever's going to be next?

Saturn, Saturn,
The planet with the rings.
Saturn, Saturn,
Is Saturn the queen . . . or maybe the king?

Jupiter, Jupiter,
The giant of the lot.
Jupiter, Jupiter,
Find out if it's cold . . . or could it be hot?

Mars, Mars,
The quite cold, giant rock.
Mars, Mars,
Are there aliens . . . or are we being mocked?

Uranus, Uranus,
The first planet discovered.
Uranus, Uranus,
Is it rock or is it . . . gas covered?

Earth, Earth,
That's where we live.
Earth, Earth,
Many thanks we take and give!

Lydia Colton (11)
Holmes Chapel Comprehensive School

A Sherbet Lemon

It is very bright and yellow,
It is smooth around the outside,
But bumpy on the top and bottom and also very sticky.

It smells like a cupful of lemon juice,
It is kind of an oval shape,
It is also symmetrical.

It looks really tasty,
It is really yummy,
It tastes all tangy from the sherbet.

It is getting smaller and smaller,
It's going smooth all over,
It's fizzy in the mouth.

Mmmmm I want another one!

Georgia Hammond (11)
Holmes Chapel Comprehensive School

THE CUPBOARD OF SECRETS

I will put in the cupboard of secrets . . .
An everlasting life for those who want it,
A world where nothing goes bad or wrong,
A heart made of crystal with the power of all love.

I will put in the cupboard of secrets . . .
A drop of water from a wonderful waterfall,
A box with all the bad of the world locked
With one hundred different padlocks and no key,
The last leaf to fall to the floor,
The first memory of a child,
The first ever star to shoot across the sky.

I will change the world by . . .
Taking away all the bad until no need for any emergency numbers,
Make everyone loved not lonely,
Make sure that everyone is treated the same.

I will make everyone imagine the perfect world
Until it becomes reality.

Sophie Illman (11)
Holmes Chapel Comprehensive School

MY MUM

M y mum is kind and thoughtful,
Y ou always know what she's thinking by the expression
on her face.

M akes sure I'm OK when I'm ill,
U sually helps me when I'm stuck with something,
M akes me a hot drink on a night when it is cold and dark.

Laura Hart (11)
Holmes Chapel Comprehensive School

Dogs

Barking at burglars like a huge shield,
Non independent - showing love for people,
Thousands of breeds, breeding more,
Eating, jumping and love makes the family dog.

Hunting and snarling like a wild bear,
Murdering innocent animals,
Chasing cats, going wild,
All these put together makes the hunting dog.

Golden retrievers and schnauzers too,
English setters and big Great Danes,
These are some breeds, there are more I know,
Take Labradors for an example too.

Dogs are all different, as you may have noticed,
There are thousands of breeds going around,
They're non independent, they show love for all,
But they can act in different sorts of their own ways.

James Pearse (11)
Holmes Chapel Comprehensive School

Alan Smith

He's white, like a hopeful and passionate player,
He's the beginning of spring all fired up,
He always wants to be there in the action,
He is the wind, gentle or furious, wanting to do something all the time,
He will be a normal person away from the action trying to chill,
He will be a medal, proud to play for his beam,
He will be a live football match on Sky Sports,
There will be a glass of Lucozade sitting on every table
giving him energy.

Oliver Jefferies (11)
Holmes Chapel Comprehensive School

SCHOOL

I set my alarm for 7am,
I like getting up early I think it's great,
It takes me a few minutes to get ready,
But I have to make sure I am not late.

The other day I nearly missed the bus,
I was in such a race,
Halfway down the road
I realised I'd forgotten my pencil case.

When I'm on the bus
I think I look a real fool,
I hate wearing the uniform
Just for one day at school.

When I arrive at school
I get ready for my first class.
When I need the loo
I always forget my hall pass.

For my homework I have to write a poem,
But I think that playing would be better,
Then I go to bed and set my alarm for 7am,
Ready for the day to start all over again.

Tom Wildman (11)
Holmes Chapel Comprehensive School

TIN OF THOUGHTS

I will put in my tin
A bright cloak made of sequins,
A multicoloured horse leaping over a meadow of poppies,
The breath of a cold, white ghost,
A slice of fresh, white cloud,
The last words of a dead celebrity.

I will put in my tin
The end of a rainbow shipped straight from the sky,
The first breath of a newborn kitten,
The last cheery laugh of Father Christmas,
The last leaf to fall in autumn.

Jenny Allen (12)
Holmes Chapel Comprehensive School

THE AMAZING SUITCASE

I will put in the suitcase

A planet of goodness and hope,
All things I know and love,
1,000,000 wishes to use to help.

I will put in the suitcase

A pair of magical football boots that never loses,
The last moments of a dying sun,
A lifetime of youth.

I will put in the suitcase

A time machine to right past wrongs,
A second chance for all the people who are ill or poor,
The world as the Garden of Eden.

I will put in the suitcase

The pride of a young boy as he lives his dream,
The strength and goodness of a human soul,
All our dreams coming true.

Christopher Harvey (11)
Holmes Chapel Comprehensive School

THE END

In the land of Mordor
The bowels of Mount Doom
Lived a large, scary creature
In the mist and the gloom.

His skin was red like burning Hell,
His eyes were black, ashes of the dead,
His claws were clear, clear as crystal,
Like a sickening virus, his evil would spread.

That night he would set off into the night sky
Not knowing, not caring if he would make children cry,
He would fly, glide and mutter every stride,
The spawn of Satan, in all his pride.

He landed on a hill,
The dust rolled away,
He could hear the faint screams
From the old inn bay.

He slammed the door open
With a push and a pull,
Looking at the bedroom doors,
They were all booked and full.

He started climbing the stairs of doom,
He was halfway up and saw the room,
The stairs got longer and stretched a lot, lot more,
He could see a boy crying through a woodgrain door.

It was in room 103,
Just that night he had a killing spree,
He opened the door, the boy was asleep,
He scratched the boy and the blood did weep.

That was the end of the young boy's life,
He was the butter and Satan was the knife.

Louis Mitchell (11)
Holmes Chapel Comprehensive School

Music

The sound of a simple tune
Staying in your head for eternity.
I love the beat, it's like a heart pumping
With its steady rhythm, trying to reach somebody.

DJs playing on their decks,
It makes you dizzy going round and round.
Singers using their mouth as tools,
That makes the perfect sound that will shatter the mind.

Listening to music is like being in the rain,
It hits you straight away, refreshing and makes you feel good.
Music is like a hunter tracking you down,
It will find you, catch you and entrance you.

James Ridgway (11)
Holmes Chapel Comprehensive School

LOST IN TIME

'Thanks for the present,' said Jimmy Rhyme,
As he looked at his watch to tell the time,
It was quarter to ten and time for bed,
So that Jimmy could rest his sleepy head.

He woke in the morning and so it did seem;
His watch had turned into a time machine.
His room had changed, the date showed 3003,
Jimmy Rhyme could not understand what he could see!

He called for his dad and an old man appeared,
With a wrinkly face and an enormous beard.
Jimmy was frightened, could this be real he feared?
Everything around him seemed so weird!

'I want to go home
And I want to go now!
So tell me how to get out of here,
Because I don't know how.'
'Time to get up,' his mum's voice said,
As Jimmy woke up, and climbed out of bed.

Ben Bleasdale (11)
Holmes Chapel Comprehensive School

MOON

Ruling over the starry sky,
The moon moves night by night,
Round the world it moves each day,
Going faster so it can play,
Moving at its own pace,
Travelling in and out of space.

Sian Woodward (11)
Holmes Chapel Comprehensive School

The Pool Of Dreams . . .

I will put in the Pool of Dreams . . .
All the power of the world enclosed in a sparkling crystal,
A silver drop of dew on a glittering flower
And a metallic phoenix with the power of ice.

I will put in the Pool of Dreams . . .
The dream of a sleeping child on Christmas Eve,
A fairy sat astride a shooting star
And a glowing shield of love and protection.

I will put in the Pool of Dreams . . .
A cure for all diseases,
1,000 candles floating in the starry sky
And the grace of a swan as it glides across the glassy surface of a lake.

I will put in the Pool of Dreams . . .
A magical locket, that, when opened, shines a beautiful light,
Making a path to the future,
Everlasting world peace
And a determination to make the Earth a better place.

Sally-Ann Heron (11)
Holmes Chapel Comprehensive School

Conkers

Brown, shiny, hard and round.
You usually find them on the ground.
1, 2, 3, 4 bend and pick them off the floor.

Soak them, string them one by one,
I know that I will have some fun.
My friends have lots, especially Ben,
But I know my best will go to ten.

Oliver Neill (11)
Holmes Chapel Comprehensive School

A NIGHTMARE!

Riding on my bike one day,
A dog came to attack me,
I fell off and met the grey
Floor that was before me.

All the skin came off my face,
My flesh started to show!
The dog ran at a very fast pace
And bit me really slow.

Its teeth dug in really far,
I could hear my bones crack.
My leg was covered in blood like tar,
It was a horribly brutal attack.

I could hear a voice in the back of my head,
It sounded like my dad,
He told me to get out of bed,
It was a nightmare that I'd had!

Lennard Pohl (12)
Holmes Chapel Comprehensive School

SHERBET LEMON

Lumpy like a frag grenade,
Yellow as summer sun,
Oval like a rugby ball,
Sticky as glue,
Semi-translucent like an old church window,
Almost tasteless until the sherbet comes,
Mouth-watering, irresistible to crunch,
It splits up into small pieces and is gone.

William Speak (11)
Holmes Chapel Comprehensive School

My Friend's Off Her Rocker

My friend's off her rocker,
She's really, really weird,
She talks just non-stop about aliens
And an old man with a beard.

I get very confused sometimes
Like whether she lives on Earth or Mars,
Because last time she slept at my house
(Which my mum never let happen again)
She woke up at 3 in the morning
And started eating chocolate bars.

But she's my best friend,
The only one I've ever had.
She's loyal and nice to me,
Although she is a bit mad!

Hayley Sherlock (11)
Holmes Chapel Comprehensive School

A Poem About A Celeb

He is crimson like the sunset in the far west,
He'd be winter, the cold frost in the early hours of the morning,
If he was a place I would associate him with Stonehenge,
Mysterious in his own way.
His clothing would be ragged, moth-eaten and torn.
He's a storm ready to erupt,
He is a beautifully carved stool.
He is a chatty interview with Michael Parkinson.
He'd be some greasy chips slipping away in your hands.

David Beckham

Theo (12)
Holmes Chapel Comprehensive School

A Sherbet Lemon

The sherbet lemons appearance is:
As yellow as the shining sun,
The shade of a lemon itself,
Rough like the mountain ranges peaking in the distance,
Perfect for my tum!

The sherbet lemons feel is:
Rough like the grips on my shoes,
Smooth as the singing of the church choir,
Liney like the check on your blouse,
It feels so divine!

The sherbet lemons smell is:
It smells as sweet as sugar,
It's a nourishing smell,
It smells as good as a million dollars,
It smells just right!

The sherbet lemons taste is:
Tangy like sharp pins,
Sour like sweet and sour without the sweet.
A vibrant sugary taste . . .
Motionless for hours on end!

The sherbet lemon is like a never-ending beach,
I wish!

Georgia Lowe (12)
Holmes Chapel Comprehensive School

Bathtime

Tonight I had a bath,
It was so deep the bubbles came up to my chin.
The water was warm and relaxing,
As my whole body slipped in
I lay back and drifted away.

And when I woke up I found myself swimming
As a mermaid under the sea.
There were fishes, crabs and octopuses.
There were oysters dotted all over the rocks
Shimmering with light on the pearls.

Gemma Phillips (11)
Holmes Chapel Comprehensive School

The Enchanted Envelope

I will put in the envelope

The silky touch from a baby's warm hand,
A drop of hope in a Mozambique woman's eyes,
A life to last for eternity.

I will put in the envelope

A day full of fun,
The last kiss of a loved one,
A kitten playing with a ball of string.

I will put in the envelope

The smell from the reddest rose in the garden of Eve,
All the happy dreams for the world to see,
Money enough to give everyone a chance.

I will put in the envelope
The happiest laugh ever laughed,
The smoothest phoenix feather,
The lights and colours of a rainbow.

My envelope is made of the shiniest fabric
With shimmers of hope in the corners,
With every type of stone,
Rubies, diamonds and sapphires decorating the sides.

Sally Jones (12)
Holmes Chapel Comprehensive School

GUESS WHO HE IS?

He is white (the calm colour), like when you are snug in your bed.
He is summer most of the time, like a bird in the sky.
He is a joke shop, like Fred and George Weasley.
He is the sun, like a person who is willing to help.
He is a jumper with mad colours, like the most colourful rainbow
in the world.
He is a spade scooping you out of a deep mess, like someone
in your family.
He is a pizza fully topped with different things
And each topping has different advice.
He is friendly, sometimes serious and sometimes funny.

This person is . . . Albus Dumbledore.

Mark Webb (11)
Holmes Chapel Comprehensive School

CREWE ALEX

C rewe is a small town with a big football heart.
R odney Jack is our goal scoring star.
E very home game you'll find me there.
W inning against opponents from near and far.
E njoying the game and the fresh air.

A shton is the name I wear on my shirt.
L oving the game even when standing in the rain.
E ach player finishing covered in dirt.
X -rays maybe needed to cure the pain.

Abbey Drinkwater (11)
Holmes Chapel Comprehensive School

TRIANGLE OF WISHES

In my triangle I will have
The dash of a dolphin,
A bar of never-ending chocolate,
A glint of a diamond on a baby.

In my triangle I will have
The last drop of water from the last lake for a dying man,
First love of everyone,
Smile of an animal.

In my triangle I will have
The first sparkle from an eye,
The firework to happiness,
The warmth from a cold place.

Hannah Roberts (12)
Holmes Chapel Comprehensive School

CHRISTMAS

C hristmas crackers popping everywhere!
H oliday madness in the air!
R ed wrapping paper piling in the bin!
I cicles as sharp as a pin!
S now as cold as ice!
T he lights like eyes of mice!
M iniature Santa on the ledge!
A little squirrel on the hedge!
S anta's on his way, hurray!

Becky Rutter (11)
Holmes Chapel Comprehensive School

The Fountain Of Dreams

My fountain will contain
A lovely silver pony grazing on the grass.
My fountain will contain
For me a lovely sister.
My fountain will contain
Primary schools all over the world.
My fountain will contain
Sports all over the world.
My fountain will contain
Peace all over the world.
My fountain will contain
The real truth about things.
My fountain will contain
No more terrorist attacks.
My fountain will contain
A love for all animals.
My fountain will contain
These wishes to come true.

Jessica Puffer (11)
Holmes Chapel Comprehensive School

Ahhhhhh!

As I come to the top
I start to shriek,
Do I tell them to stop?
I am clinging onto my friend
And she said,
'It's not scary.'
We're there now,
You can open your eyes now.

Kelsey Tinker (12)
Holmes Chapel Comprehensive School

My Mystical Chest

I will put in my chest
The roar of a powerful engine,
The rumble of thunder in the distance,
The friendly bark of a gentle dog.

The first goal on match day,
The first twist of a throttle on a new motorbike,
The phone ringing when a friend calls.

The day racism ends,
The day war is no more,
The day terrorism dies.

Daniel French (12)
Holmes Chapel Comprehensive School

Windermere

W ater is icy cold.
I n my wetsuit I swim.
N o one can get me out of the water.
D inner in the caravan.
E very time I swim, I snorkel.
R ubber dingy rowing is harder than it looks.
M any fish around my feet.
E veryone watches me as I jump off the jetty.
R eally having fun,
E njoying every minute.

Sammy Cooper (11)
Holmes Chapel Comprehensive School

Stop And Start

As I reached the top
My ears began to pop
And my heart wouldn't stop.

As it suddenly started
Me and my breath parted
When I finally farted.

Chris Pilling (12)
Holmes Chapel Comprehensive School

Roller Coaster!

Crack! Crack!
Goes the sound of the track,
We get to the top,
See the very large drop,
My stomach was churning,
People's heads were turning,
We dropped, we screamed.

Ashleigh Parsons (12)
Holmes Chapel Comprehensive School

Wind

The wind beats down
On the spindly trees.
It makes them suffer
More than their stout cousins.
Wind is a real brute,
There is nowhere to hide.

James Smith (11)
Holmes Chapel Comprehensive School

The Bottle Of Dreams

In my bottle I will put
The golden feather of a phoenix,
The magic of a dream,
A unicorn galloping
Through the woods.
In my bottle I will put
The first bite of chocolate,
A serum for invincibility,
A way to bring the deceased back to life.
In my bottle I will put
Eternal youth,
The gateway to Heaven
And the meaning of life.

James Rickelton (12)
Holmes Chapel Comprehensive School

The Fat Cow

The fat cow has a really big udder
And it has a tendency to shudder.

The fat cow's belly touches the ground,
But it wasn't like that when it was found.

The fat cow has a number on its butt
And down the middle it has a big cut.

The fat cow was late
And now its leg is on my plate.

Chris Martin (11)
Holmes Chapel Comprehensive School

Let Me Run Far Away

Give me chance to escape,
Let me run far away.
Find me somewhere to hide,
If only for a day.

Let the sun cast its shadows,
Let the moon light the sky.
Faded like a fallen star,
You'll never see me cry.

Let me drown in an ocean,
Let me dance in the sun.
Until I see you coming
And know it's time to run.

Like a broken angel,
Let me lie in the dust.
Shattered dreams and twisted lies,
Betrayal and mistrust.

Scared to look inside myself,
Who knows what I shall find?
Make me rise from my knees,
Scare these thoughts from my mind.

Leave me for now,
Let me run far away.
Let me hide myself behind you,
Just for one more day.

Kristina Daniels (14)
Loreto Grammar School

THE SCHOOL STREAK

Break into school
Of a student into trouble
Enter detention

We shall not be moved
Or else I shall fall to my knees
And beg the teacher

Maths is so boring
We have to do some adding
Like what's two times?

My friend Ethel told me
There's a streak at school
I told her, 'Don't look.'

'Yeah,' I said to her,
'Don't look Ethel.'
It was too late, she already looked

Well, yes, it's a streak
Oh boy! Oh boy! Oh boy! Ooh!
That's really too much

People were laughing
At him 'cause he crashed into the wall
I'm laughing as well.

Sarah Brown (14)
Ryles Park High School

THE SEA

Stone-cold ebbs and flows,
Comes and goes with highs and lows,
Ever flows the sea.

Shimmering, glistening,
In the sunrays,
Looking back on old summer days.

Jumping, splashing in the water,
Surfing, sailing,
Loads to do,
This is the sea.

Maisie Burrows (11)
Ryles Park High School

FOOTBALL!

Crowds cheer and then celebrate with beer
When you see your team winning
It is just like you are dreaming.
When I see United play
We always trash and bash the other team away.
When I see David Beckham have a bash
I know he will always smash the score.
Even if United don't win the league
We will always see United flying high.

Chris Longden (12)
Ryles Park High School

In My Soul

I went down the road
to see if the dream was real
I saw the one thing that I would like
to have one day in my life
I have spent my whole life looking for love
but I never thought it could hurt this much
I would love to feel some peace
in my soul
I would like to rest in peace
from all the torture I have lived with
all my life.

Robert Farr (15)
Ryles Park High School

My Pet Dog

I have a pet dog with floppy ears,
He's been with us for years and years.
His name is Fred, which rhymes with Ted
And at night he likes to sleep warm in his bed
With his paws on his head.
At the break of dawn he has a yawn
And then goes and runs around the lawn.
When I'm mad he goes all sad,
But that's my pet dog Fred.

Danny Hague (14)
Ryles Park High School

My Little Sister

My little sister -
I remember when she was born.
I loved her to pieces.
I never left her alone,
But now she's growing up;
I'm starting to get worried,
She's getting just as big as me
And getting what she wants.
I'm now starting to hate her;
Maybe even leave.
But that's not the worst!
She's even starting to shout!
And when I shout at her
She starts to cry.
Then I feel sorry.
My dad's going mad
But deep down inside
I love my little sister!

Stephen Barsted (15)
Ryles Park High School

Neo My Cat

Neo is my cat.
She is a little rascal,
But she is my rascal.
She has a cold,
But she loves to go out.
She likes to lick my ear.
Neo is my cat.

Sara Neild (12)
Ryles Park High School

PETS

I have a pet
It hates to get wet
It can be lazy
It goes crazy.

It likes to catch a mouse
And to lie on our couch.
It likes to fish
And eats its fish out of a dish.

It can jump up high
But can't fly
It likes our mat
That's where it's sat.

What's my pet?

It's a cat. How about that!

James Calvert (11)
Ryles Park High School

MY CAT SUKI

My cat's black and brown
And when I tell her to sit down
She sits down!
My cat sits on your back
When you tell her to get down
She wishes that she was not a cat.
My cat's just the best
When she gets told off
Oh no, a really bad stress.

Kimberley Dent (13)
Ryles Park High School

THE WORLD

The world is big
The world is small
It's like a giant shopping mall
When I eat my delight
I see the bright stars at night
When I hear the little sheep cry
I know it's time to say goodbye.

People, animals, love and hate
It's all dished out on a great big plate.

When people get high over a piece of pie
While they think of themselves like little elves
With their pointed ears
And their silly little beards.

Scott Stubbs (12)
Ryles Park High School

LOOKING THROUGH THE EYE OF SOMEONE ELSE

Thinking about it.
Look through the eye of someone else.
It would be freaky, creaky, slimy and sneaky.
Looking through the eye of someone else
Would be scary, airy, daring and baring.
But think about all the things you could see
Through the big, wide eye that would be
Twice the size of you.
It would still be freaky, creaky, slimy and sneaky,
Take this from one who knows!

Hannah King (12)
Ryles Park High School

FOOTBALL

Football is fun in the sun.
Football is mad like my dad.
I like this game because it's the same.
I strike the ball and it hits the wall.
The ball hits the net like it was set.
The fans cheer as the players near.
This game is great like the American state.
This game is brill, it gives us a thrill.
Football is sporty like Shorty.
Football is great like my mate.
I like to play every day.
I like to say I can play.
The players are grumpy as well as frumpy.
The game is tense.
This game is great but it's the refs I hate.
This game is long like Hong Kong.

Aaron Stubbs (11)
Ryles Park High School

THE SNAKE

They're slimy.
Hear them when they hiss.
Every day they hunt.

Slithering along the ground,
Nosily they warn you not to come too close.
Then attacking without warning,
Killing his prey with one bite.
Evening comes once again for another day is dawning.

Alan Roach (13)
Ryles Park High School

Siobhan's Poem

S iobhan stands for intelligent
I ntelligent stands for obsessive
O bsessive stands for bravery
B ravery stands for happy
H appy stands for angry
A ngry stands for naughty
N aughty stands for Siobhan.

Siobhan Paylor (15)
Ryles Park High School

Thomas Bennett

T om is good.
H e likes Mrs Archer,
O nly when she is nice.
M aths is bad.
A rt is good.
S ometimes I'm happy;
sometimes I'm sad.

Thomas Bennett (11)
Ryles Park High School

My Dog Tess

T ess is ten
E veryone likes her
S he does not bite
S he is Tess and she always will be.

Jake Goodwin (12)
Ryles Park High School

Storm

S tarted to blow
Chilling my spine
Blundering storm howling and screeching.

T rees slashing at my windows
Making shadows on my walls.

O pened my window, freezing air
Came rushing in like a swarm of bees,
Wind swirling in my room
Hurriedly I close the window

R ustling leaves outside
The storm had gone
The night went quiet
All was calm.

M uch better to go to sleep *zzz*.

Bruce Wilcox (10)
Ryles Park High School

Amie Regan

A mie is cool.
M usic is my best thing.
I like to dance with my friends and I
E njoy it very much.

R aving is my best thing.
E ven TV is really good.
G iant rabbits are my favourite
A nd teddies.
N ew stuff makes me happy.

Amie Regan (11)
Ryles Park High School

My Dog Molly

Molly is beautiful,
Like a shining star,
Molly is wonderful
And never goes too far.

Molly is faithful,
She loves us very much,
Molly is cuddly
And her fur is soft to touch.

Molly is playful
And always rips around,
Molly is extremely fast,
But never runs out of bounds.

Molly is noisy,
With a very loud bark,
Molly is even louder,
Than a mad lark!

Molly is sleepy,
Curled up in a ball,
Molly is comfy,
Using a cushion as a soft wall.

I would like to thank Molly (and her charm)
For helping with the inspiration of this poem.

Melissa Trueman (11)
Ryles Park High School

Seagull's Winter

The beach is bleak
Winter has my world in its grip
The cold sinks its teeth into me
I can't escape it.

No one knows
What lies beyond the horizon
I close my eyes
And long for the end.

Georgia de Vicq (13)
Ryles Park High School

A Poem For My Cousin Jamie-Lea Hitchener

Knock, knock, knock upon my door
No need to guess who it will be,
It's my best friend Jamie knocking for me.
Every morning without a doubt
She comes up the path with a great big shout.

I open the door for Jamie-Lea
Not much time to watch TV,
We're almost ready for going to school.
We get our bags and off we go
Up the street and away we go!

My best friend Jamie
Has moved away,
I really miss her
And I wanted her to stay.

I wish she'd ring
Or send a letter,
Or if she could come and see me
That would be even better.

Friends are always
Friends forever,
I'll never forget Jamie-Lea
No not ever.

Louise Murphy (11)
Ryles Park High School

Not So Amazing

Sitting here, the view's amazing,
The splash of the water against the rocks,
The pull of the waves against the pebbles and seashells,
The shade of the sand yellowy golden,
But more of a mustard colour where the waves have reached,
Little children building sandcastles, their mouths full of ice cream.

Sitting here, the view's amazing,
Adults sunbathing having a natter with their friends,
Out on the horizon cruise ships coming in
And nearer to the shore are old boats
With men fishing for their lunch and tea,
But now it's not so amazing,
Not so wonderful as it was before,
It's just me.

Stephanie Beattie (13)
Ryles Park High School

My Caravan

My caravan is lovely and clean
On the back of the car - it looks mean
The two main rooms are ours and Mum's and Dad's
They can't complain, it's just too bad
In the day it only looks small
But at night it's as big as the mall
Four bunk beds for all the kids
A big double bed - that's so big
I bang my head when I get up
Oh - no that's just my luck.

Danielle Miller (14)
Ryles Park High School

FEAR, ANGER AND END

Fear is a powerful weapon,
Fear is used against the people,
Warlords strive on this weapon,
Peace-bringers can never bear it,
Fear makes people feel trapped and scared,
The fear machine eats people alive and never takes any prisoners,
Fear is a pit of fiery hell with no end . . .
Anger brings the attack,
Anger brings the death,
Anger brings the war,
Anger is what we feel,
Anger is what we have against the religious warlord,
Anger is a colossal force that can never end . . .
End is what we want,
End is what we hate,
End is what we fear,
End is what must come,
End is something dangerous,
End can become redemption,
End is the end.
The end.

Wayne Woodward (13)
Ryles Park High School

MY LOVE

Love - What is love?
Love is that silly thing
That warms your heart.
It's the last thing you think of at night.
I have someone to love
Do you?

Faith Brooks (14)
Ryles Park High School

LIFE

If you were me
And I were you
What would life be?
Singing and shouting
Flying in the sky
Jumping up and down
Rolling under the hill
Growing time by time
You
Me
Him

You and me
Out and in
Up and down
Moving time by time
Eat and drink
High and low
Light and dark
Me and you.

Heidi Band (13)
Ryles Park High School

THE SCHOOL TRIP

I went on a school trip
To Chester zoo,
We saw all the monkeys
Doing a poo!

We went to seals
And then the giraffes,
We saw the hyenas
Which made us laugh.

We got on the coach
To go back home,
What an enjoyable day
Now go to sleep!

Oli Rayner (14)
Ryles Park High School

WHAT AM I?

I am a scare,
So beware,
I brighten up the night,
It might give you a fright.

Sometimes I come without a sound,
Sometimes I might shake the rotten ground,
I come out quick,
Like a flying brick.

Some people may fear me,
I shine with fear vividly,
You may have a shiver,
To even make you quiver.

I am your fear,
But then I'll disappear,
Until another stormy day,
Don't bother to beg or pray.

What am I?
I am lightning.

Christopher Plant (11)
Ryles Park High School

Colours

C olours are the happiest thing to be.
O ver the rainbow, over you and me.
L ighten up my darkest nights.
O therwise, all gone and out of sight.
U nderneath the rainbow, I see you all.
R are and grow so tall.
S ee you all, beautiful colours!

Joanna Worthington (16)
Ryles Park High School

Music!

M usic makes your feet dance
U ltimate rhythm pulsing through your body
S ongs to go with the music that moves you
I n cases of emergency press *'play'*
'C ause the music will get your heart pumping!

Sarah Bentley (13)
Ryles Park High School

My Dog Misty

M y name is Misty.
I love my family dearly.
S tretchy toys are good for a game.
T ia and Mia are my two best buds.
Y ou see I have lots of friends and my family,
they love me.

Sarah Huxley (14)
Ryles Park High School

Kim Huxley

K ims are good.
I like dogs.
M ia, Misty and Tia are my dogs' names.

H orses are cute.
U gly people are annoying.
X mas is coming.
L ions are in the zoo.
E lephants are there too.
Y ours sincerely.

Kimberley Huxley (11)
Ryles Park High School

Friends

My mates are my friends
Who come round and I play with,
But most of all my best friend is my mum.
She loves me and cares for me
And listens to what I say.
She's my best friends.

Deborah Plant (14)
Ryles Park High School

My Dog

H ow much do I love my dog?
O ne in a million.
N ow and then he can get on my nerves.
E very night I take my dog for a walk.
Y es - my dog is one in a million.

Jade McDonald (13)
Ryles Park High School

THE MURDER

My house is a sight
My face turns bright
I see lots of police cars

I also spot a body
A body of my friend
I look at him and cry

The SWAT team tell me
A murderer killed my friend
And they all go and find the murderer

I hear the sirens of the police cars and SWAT vans
They head to jail along with the FBI
The murderer has been captured

I hear my mother telling me to come inside
Because she has a little surprise for me
I have a new girlfriend named Susan

Then Susan and I go out together
To shops and other places
And that is my interesting day.

Luke Edwards (14)
Ryles Park High School

SPONTANEOUS COMBUSTION

Burnt alive or hit by cars,
I always dream about pop stars.

Talentless, manufactured on TV,
Crushing all metal band's dreams.

Metal music will never see an end
But pop stars will be labelled as a passing trend.

All my life I've carried the scar
Of hating all manufactured pop stars.

Joe Swift (15)
Ryles Park High School

MOTOR VEHICLES

Motors are big, motors are small,
You could get a motor that powers a ball.
I've got a motorbike which goes really fast,
I would ride and ride it and I'd go whizzing past.
My motorbike is big, it is white and blue,
I can go really fast, I will prove it to you.

A quad bike it will go ninety miles an hour,
The quad bike has lots and lots of power.
Our quad has 28 horse power, it can pull a trailer.
It will even pull a bailer.

My car, my car I have my own car,
My car is a van and it has no bull bar.
My van is good and will go really fast,
This van of mine should really last and last.

Our tractors are good, our tractors are brill,
Tractors will drive over a landfill.
They will not get stuck if you drive through a bog,
Tractors, tractors, they drive on a cog.
Vehicles always give me a thrill.

Daniel Turnock (12)
Ryles Park High School

My Dog Pip

Pip is the dog who always eats the strangest thing!
Like socks and shoes
And mats and rats and
Even the cats think he's weird.

Pip the dog is a terrible rebel
No wonder his owners call him trouble.
He always seems to do the doggy run.
My dog Pip the naughty one.

I even chased him along the canal then ended up at Astra Zeneca.
I think I deserve a medal for my efforts with
This terror,
Pip, my dog.

Stephen Ash (13)
Ryles Park High School

Friends

F riends will always be there for you no matter what is going on.
R ight or wrong they will stick by you.
I f you are upset they will cheer you up.
E verything you tell your friends you can trust them not to tell anyone else.
N othing you do or say can make your friends hate you.
D on't ever fall out with your friends if you do you will have no one.
S ometimes friends will let you down but you will always forgive them.

You see friends are forever.

Kim Adams (13)
Ryles Park High School

When

When the moon shines on my bedroom wall,
When everyone looks at me
When you read this letter you will think of me
When people stop and stare I think of you
When you kiss me good night, I feel the love in my heart
When I think of you every night
I want to kiss you good night!

Samantha Kingdon (12)
Ryles Park High School

Star, Star

Star, star where are you,
I wonder what you would do.
I look up into the sky
And wonder why and what you do.

In winter you gave me a beautiful sight.
Stars shine brightly in the sky.

Chantelle Pelka (12)
Ryles Park High School

The Sun

The sun is hot.
I like to play
On the beach, in the sea
I like to play in the sand
To dig holes so people fall in.
When the ice cream man comes to the beach
I get a chocolate ice cream and it melts in my hand.

Craig Davies (13)
Ryles Park High School

THE PATH

The dark path,
It pulls me in,
I do not want to,
It would be a sin.

The dust lying still,
Sacred, untouched,
I try to repel,
But it's just too much.

Those hanging trees,
That mystery,
All the different things
I want to see.

That teasing lane,
It drew me inside,
For from my want,
I could no longer hide.

I regret that day,
I loath it I say,
For I knew, even then,
That I would have to pay.

Pay for those leaves,
Pay for that dust,
But pay most of all,
For saying, 'I must.'

I must lay my eyes,
On that treasure despise,
All of those warnings,
Of unwoken mornings.

An unwoken morning,
I yearn for the day,
Anything's better,
Than having to stay.

Always dreary,
Dark and weary,
Through the trees I steer,
But they never clear.

I have the endless task
Of trying to escape,
But I fear to do that,
More than a lifetime it shall take.

Anna Perry (11)
Ryles Park High School

Books

Books are great!
Books are funny and sad,
Fiction and non-fiction
They are all great no matter what.
Books are like subtle knives
They cut through worlds into my mind
With dragons and unicorns and wizards
It's all there
Just waiting for you
To open them.

Joseph Gilbert (11)
Ryles Park High School

FISHING

I set my tackle up with rods and reels.
I wait and wait for a big bite.
Then I get one, it's only small,
But it's better than nothing at all.
I cast back in right across the river
And it goes all quiet, once again.
I wait and wait, I throw some maggots in,
Hoping that it will be a big bite.
Then I have something, I think it's a big one, yes,
It is, it must be a one and a half pounder.
We pack up, with me very glad
With my catch of the day.

Chris Heapy (11)
Ryles Park High School

WHO?

When I heard she was dead,
I banged my head,
She was the best thing I had,
But I treated her bad,
I tried my hardest to treat her right,
But now she's dead and it was at night,
But now she's gone
My favourite bun,
My mum said, 'Don't worry,
I will get you another bunny.'

Terry Winchester (13)
Ryles Park High School

Cats And Dogs

Cats and dogs always squabble.
Always fighting over my bobble.
Ripping curtains,
Smashing plates,
That's cats and dogs,
They can never be mates.

When you're in bed,
They're near your head.
Looking in your eyes,
Thinking of pork pies.
Crunch, crunch, crunch,
Munch, munch, munch.

Jessica Bebbington (11)
Ryles Park High School

Safe

It's a cold, black night,
The wind howls down the chimney,
The rain lashes on the window,
Lightning blindly fills the sky,
Thunder rumbles deafeningly.
The logs on the fire crackle,
The flames glow red and orange,
The heat burns my face,
But I'm safe inside,
Warm and dry.

Alex Terry (13)
Ryles Park High School

Lurve Poem!

Only I know what love is because I have found love,
That was the other day now,
That love has gone.
It hasn't come back yet,
I hope it will come back some day soon.

I'll have to find that love in someone else.
I really miss that love feeling.

Tell me, have you ever felt love?

Natalie Heywood (11)
Ryles Park High School

Winter

At last! Winter's just round the corner,
You can make so many things out of snow,
Especially the crazy snowball fights,
Constructing snowmen is always the best.
Sledging's brilliant! You have to try it!
Sliding down a snowy hillside is fun,
Inside the houses, Christmas lights sparkle,
Decorating the tree is excellent,
Waking up on Christmas morning is great,
Rushing downstairs to open your presents,
Going to mass to celebrate Jesus,
Sharing Christmas dinner with family,
Eventually Christmas dies away
And now to prepare for the new year.

Mark Roberts (11)
St Nicholas RC High School, Hartford

SPRING

Pink flowers are growing, spring is coming,
Trees are blossoming, leaves start to appear,
Small lambs are being born, birds are singing,
Winter fades, in the sun runs a wild deer,
Rabbits are digging their burrows in the ground,
Fluffy yellow chicks scattering around,
In the fresh air is a beautiful sound,
Easter will soon come, chocolate eggs are found,
April showers beating on the pier,
Children splash in puddles, next to the bay,
Soon it will end and summer will draw near,
Foals and calves will grow bigger and older,
Nothing can compare to a spring morning,
Now it's time for summer, sun is shining.

Kathryn Andrews (11)
St Nicholas RC High School, Hartford

WINTER SONNET

Santa puts the presents under the tree,
As excited boys and girls run downstairs,
Happy faces glow, they're filled with glee,
They have received toy cars and teddy bears,
Bright glowing lights all round the busy town,
Armies of snowmen stand and wait in snow,
The atmosphere brings a smile not a frown,
The icy cold wind of winter is here,
Cold dark nights draw in quicker, chilled winds blow,
Children wrap up because the cold is near,
Frost is glistening on the car window,
Puddles freeze over and turn to crystal
And the rain sounds like a shooting pistol.

Rebecca Carroll (11)
St Nicholas RC High School, Hartford

Autumn Cheer

The hot summer is gone,
The autumn is here to bring us a big cheer,
It is a peaceful day,
The leaves are falling softly off the trees,
The wind whistles a tune,
The squirrels in the trees come out to play.

There is then a bright light,
The sun fights his way through the tall trees,
The squirrels run blindly,
The cold weather has gone, the sun has heat,
The sun puts on his coat,
The wind is angry, he blows really hard.

The sun is defeated,
All the animals come out of their hiding,
For winter they prepare,
The sun is thankfully gone,
'Phew,' says the wind,
All the animals praise him,
Let's all rejoice with a very big cheer.

Rachael McCooey (11)
St Nicholas RC High School, Hartford

Spring Sonnet

Buds pushing through the hard, frosty ground,
Snowdrops heads are swaying in the warm breeze,
New life - the cycle is coming around,
Sweet birdsong is being heard in the trees,
New life awakened eggs are being laid,
Plants offering their sweet, scented flowers,
New leaves and buds on the trees are being made,
Mother Nature showing her true powers.

Animals waking, fruit and nuts are ate,
Bunnies are hopping on the new, fresh grass,
The berries on the trees are staying late,
People are celebrating while at mass,
The morning sun rises on a new day,
Spring: the season where children come and play.

Sophie Crooks (11)
St Nicholas RC High School, Hartford

WINTER IS HERE

Leaves falling on the ground,
The colours are beginning to be found,
Yellow, brown, orange, green,
Covering the path that cannot be seen,
With leaves the children play,
They all wrap up warm and have fun all day.

Heavy winds start blowing
And it has suddenly started snowing,
The sky has got no sun,
Winter and autumn, the battle's begun,
Seasons thrashing it out,
Winter's won the battle without a doubt.

Outside, starting to snow,
Big strong heavy winds are starting to grow,
Out in the freezing cold,
All the colours of the world are now bold,
All the fields are white
And in the morning the sun is not bright.

Sophie Gregory (11)
St Nicholas RC High School, Hartford

WINTER TIME

Snow's coming, getting near,
Animals hibernate, battle is here,
Days go dark, nights are cold,
Autumn's now ending and the trees are gold,
Winter's upon us now,
In from the fields come sheep and cows.

All the grass has turned white
And all the trees look like they're out of sight,
Heavy winds start to come
And all of the snow has come and begun,
Everything starts to freeze
And now I will be the heavy breeze.

Heavy winds have been growing
And all the new grass has started showing,
Leaves are white on the trees,
The winds have frozen them with bitter ease,
How much more can we take,
Until the spring chases Jack Frost away?

Emma Archbold (12)
St Nicholas RC High School, Hartford

SUMMER - THE SEA

A cold blue sea sends a chill up my back
Speedboats race, churning up waves sending ripples,
Nearby scarlet poppies fill the green fields,
Animals shade the blistering sun,
I soon notice the gentle summer rain,
In the hot sun people are sunbathing,
Lying like lizards on the yellow sand,
Manipulating their skin to chocolate.

The sun will soon be covered quicker
And people will feel winter's cold grip,
Giving them fevers and making them cold
And they won't have sun burn but frost bite,
The days won't be hot when they crave water,
Soon they will be craving fire in the season of winter.

Laurence Lewis (12)
St Nicholas RC High School, Hartford

SUMMER'S CRY

Summer's dreading the autumn,
Why can't it just be summer all the time?
Why are we being cursed?
Why is summer in chains, why? Please help us,
Why can't autumn leave now?
Go away autumn, we need summer, not you.

Summer is melting away,
Autumn should just be struck down by lightning,
Summer's fading away,
Summer can't cope, autumn please melt away,
Autumn leaves us alone,
Summer's going and everyone's crying.

Now that summer's fading
And autumn's coming ahead, on its way,
The leaves are dropping down,
Now everyone is sinking from summer,
Please just stay, summer please,
The summer's teardrops, like sharp icicles.

Rachael Achilles (12)
St Nicholas RC High School, Hartford

Winter Blunders

Autumn has now ended,
The leaves still scattered tell a tale of battle,
Every hour gets darker,
Winter arrives in style shaking crusty snow,
Everywhere is covered,
Wildly expressing his territory.

Winter, making it the best,
Brushing snow everywhere,
Winter has won,
Winter the white season,
Autumn's revenge begun,
Autumn's evil eye on winter season,
Winter stands over his victory.

Autumn, hiding, plotting,
No one knows when he'll strike for victory,
Winter still holding on,
Autumn strikes, sweeping the brow a natural brush,
Winter has won for good,
Autumn, his own army lost the battle.

Jodie Frazer (11)
St Nicholas RC High School, Hartford

My Winter Sonnet

The snow falls creating a white blanket,
The rain splutters on the bare, icy trees,
Icicles hang off the eaves of the roof,
The dead plants are covered with snow and ice,
The pond has frozen, ducks are ice skating,
Sleepy animals have hibernated,
The long, dark nights become bitter and bleak,
Dew drops fall on the frosty spiderwebs.

Choose a Christmas tree with pungent pine scent,
Discover dusty boxes in the loft,
Untangling the lights and trying them out,
The shining baubles glisten in the light,
Children leaving stockings for Santa Claus,
Leave a mince pie and carrot for Rudolph.

Rebecca Chorlton (12)
St Nicholas RC High School, Hartford

Autumn The Devil - Why?

Autumn the devil - why?
All the effort I put into myself,
Goes because of autumn,
Every year the same when it comes again,
It's in hell, why autumn?
Leave me alone I want to be on my own.

Many a day I try,
All I want is to be shot and die,
I carry around blessings,
You carry around the devil in hand,
Watching the leaves drop down,
Can't you see here, that you are killing me.

I will fight back I will not lose to you,
Autumn you're nearly here,
I'm fading away, autumn cos you're here,
Now that I am dying,
I'll come back next year and try to slay you,
Autumn the devil - why?

Emily Faint (11)
St Nicholas RC High School, Hartford

SEPARATE SEASONS

Autumn tells the leaves
'Change colour and fall.'
The leaves steadily drop,
Yellows, browns and reds all mixed together,
The trees are arguing with winter frost,
The war is beginning.

The frost grabs hold of the trees and shakes hard,
The trees are groaning, 'Help!'
The frost laughing as he freezes all streams,
Nothing is spared by frost,
He is supreme ruler of winter days,
Frost has taken over.

Animals run away from the coldness,
Winter's army has come,
But spring will come and take over winter,
His sword will slash winter,
He will be gone for now, but will return,
All is restored with spring.

Jonathon Vale (11)
St Nicholas RC High School, Hartford

A SPRING POEM

Spring is the most colourful period,
With lots of animals being new born,
The plants are waking and growing quickly,
Snow is melting and the sun is shining,
Everyone in the land is kissing,
Winter is now gone, leaving no remains,
With flowers blooming and cattle grazing,
My favourite time is finally here.

It seems that there is always a drizzle,
It is still cold and it gets through my coat,
The foxes are always eating the sheep,
I like to jump in all of the big puddles,
I get my sister wet and my mum too,
Thick dark mists cover over my round eyes.

Joe Grzywinski (11)
St Nicholas RC High School, Hartford

SUMMER'S HERE!

The spring's gone, summer's here,
The world is full of beautiful flowers,
The trees are a lovely green,
The sparkling sand is golden yellow,
The sea is a deep green,
The sky is diamond blue with silver clouds.

The sun opens her eyes,
She welcomes the world with beams of daylight,
She glistens on the sea,
The sand starts to blush when they see her face,
She's like a buzzy bee,
Working all day and night for you and me!

Now the summer is here,
The sun gives off her dazzling light beams,
The spring is very cross,
She really tries to defeat the summer!
The spring's gone, summer's here!
Let's all rejoice with a very big cheer!

Hannah Smith (11)
St Nicholas RC High School, Hartford

AUTUMN THE BOSS

The sun is happy now,
Don't let autumn take over, how, why, how?
The battle has begun,
Think about sun, sand, sea, ice cream and fun,
The smile on your face,
Don't, don't, don't let me turn into autumn.

This bit is about me,
Leaves falling on the floor, I'm better see,
Red, brown all on the floor,
I am more interesting you see lots more!
Every colour that is here,
Have fallen from the tree alone, dead tree.

In the end after that,
One will win, the over swept under the mat,
When summer comes again,
Which will control the cold and the wet rain,
Main star in my world,
Who turns everything from very warm to *dead!*

Katharine Hough (11)
St Nicholas RC High School, Hartford

WINTER

It's getting colder, winter's in the air,
People are having snowball fights outside,
Children are going to the Christmas fair,
Snow crunches under your feet when you walk,
Relatives come over to celebrate,
Fogies sit by fires and have a talk,
Fires are blazing with bright white lights,

Presents are wrapped with shiny new paper
And high quality ribbons hold them tight,
3 more seconds to go, 2 getting close,
1, 'Happy New Year everyone!'
We have a roast, carrots, cauliflower
And stuffing full of loads of herbs and spices,
I cannot wait until the next winter!

Mark Lawrenson (11)
St Nicholas RC High School, Hartford

SUMMER POEM

The heat was hard to take,
It was like a volcano erupting,
It was like a boiler,
I would do anything for a cold drink,
By this time, it was hell,
I wanted to sit on a block of ice.

This sun was beating me,
Like a commando in the US army,
The sun was a devil,
It was torturing me every day,
The sun like chilli,
Was the hottest chilli in the world.

Autumn was arriving,
Summer was ready for autumn's coming,
They battled and battled,
Until autumn won and the leaves fell,
Now autumn rules the land,
Like a king with his country that he owns.

Laurence Norman (11)
St Nicholas RC High School, Hartford

UP, UP, UP AND THEN DOWN

Up, up, up and then down,
Winter has come, to declare the cold war,
Wind will shout through the leaves,
Time has come for you to freeze for the year,
The wind has stung the leaves,
Time has come, the battle has just begun.

Winter will draw forever,
Autumn will dawn forever, autumn is best,
You won't win for the year,
Autumn will defend and will keep its toll,
You might have won for now,
Autumn will see you in the great battle.

Marching for the last time,
Rustling for the future and with pride,
Clash, rip and screams to death,
The wind will crush you down like elephants,
Wind has stood its own ground,
Battle was over before it started.

Neil Cripps (11)
St Nicholas RC High School, Hartford

SONNET

Autumn is good for a relaxing breeze,
People working on their harvest for food,
The orangy leaves blow around the street,
While the farmers are gathering their wheat,
Autumn has beautiful colours to see,
The brown branches stand up against the sky,
Autumn seems to last a very long time,

People work in the fields all day long,
Birds in their nests singing their songs,
Dark closes in to leave objects' shadows,
The curtains are drawn, and the lights are on,
It's harder to get up in the morning,
My eyes are glued, I want to go to sleep,
There are two sides to autumn, good and bad.

Ross James Adamson (11)
St Nicholas RC High School, Hartford

SPRING VICTORY AND DEFEAT

Spring drew one last blow,
Frost was dead, his ice minions gone,
Green leaves like soldiers sprung,
Up from their ice graves alive,
Fish set free from ice cages,
Spring's army had come. Spring ruled *all!*

He was serenaded,
Spring was king supreme! Colours announced his glory.
Rich colours like gold,
Spring was richer than any king.
Spring had built a barrier,
Ready for Summer hoping he would live.

Then waited in vain,
For the coming of Summer meant battle!
Leaves like swords were made,
Sharpened, given to each tree in turn,
Summer came! The swords clashed.
Spring had drawn his last breath,
Summer had won.

Liam Hickson (11)
St Nicholas RC High School, Hartford

AUTUMN BATTLES SUMMER

Autumn battles summer,
Summer is dreading the dark, wet autumn,
Every year they battle,
Autumn wants rid of the warm, sunny days,
The sun battles hard rain,
The wet weather crunches the light bright sun.

The sun is glistening bright,
It is very happy with its gold sands,
It knows autumn will come,
The sun wants to beat the black, dark autumn,
The sun likes its brightness,
The sun battles the hard, dark, wet autumn.

The autumn has gold leaves,
It likes the darkness and the wet weather,
Autumn likes the battle,
The autumn likes the long and dark battle,
Autumn fights long and hard,
The gold leaves are dancing with joyfulness.

Grace Davies (11)
St Nicholas RC High School, Hartford

AUTUMN

Crinkled up leaves fall gently to the ground,
Bare trees have been stripped of their coat of leaves,
Scattered outside, animals can be found,
Then throughout the light snow I can see a grave,
The earth is harvesting for the new spring,
Taking seeds, nursing and caring for them,
Birds fly around with their swift little wings,
Outside the entire world is a bright gem,

A golden sun shines down onto the earth,
In bright fields there's colours everywhere,
All around there's a great look of new birth,
It's a picture that you would like to share,
Autumn is a season full of surprise,
But the best thing is the autumn sunrise,
Letting its sun shine down on everything.

Sean McMahon (11)
St Nicholas RC High School, Hartford

Spring Sonnet

The early spring mornings with gleaming grass,
All the buds come out on the empty trees,
The fresh flowers sway in the morning breeze,
The frost fades away while the sun shines out.

Cute, young, fluffy animals prance about
New birds chirping all day wanting more food,
Their small, soft feathers helping them to fly,
The squirrels, the hedgehogs and mice come out.

Pink blossom falls down like snow in the breeze,
All the plants grow lots of new lovely fresh buds,
There are poppies, daisies and tulips too,
The lovely smell from the flowers spread around.

Spring is good, it's like a new beginning,
It's the brightest time of all the year.

Helena Saunders-Lee (11)
St Nicholas RC High School, Hartford

Spring Sonnet

Winter is over, spring has just begun,
A new life blossomed in the golden sun,
Trees are showing their beautiful green leaves,
Song birds are singing their little hearts out,
Flowers are out, beautiful in colour,
Daffodils dance as the meadows prosper,
Lambs are showing their beautiful white coats,
Gambolling playfully, with frolicking jumps,
Snowdrops, new life, pushing up through the earth,
Spring holds a promise for new beginnings,
April showers drench and flood out the region,
No more flood plains, no rhyme nor reason,
Easter is coming, very soon after,
Spring will end and the summer will begin.

Niall Ellis-Patterson (11)
St Nicholas RC High School, Hartford

Sonnet On Winter

Icy winds freezing everything they touch,
Thousands of small snowflakes starting to fall,
Slippery ice being covered by white snow,
Strong, watery wind being blown in your face,
Cursing your car as it skids in thick ice,
Children laughing s they throw wet snowballs,
Icy cold water running down their tops,
Turning it into a crazy snow fight,
Mums in houses making sweet Christmas pud,
The smell of roast turkey filling the air,
Children posting letters to Santa Claus,
While red stockings hang by the blazing fire,
Bright Christmas tree lights hung up everywhere,
Everyone wanting presents of some kind.

Rosemary Phillips (11)
St Nicholas RC High School, Hartford

AUTUMN

The soft, golden brown leaves sink to the ground,
As the sweet sound of children fills the air
And they start to play conker fights with joy,
The kids start to buy their scary costumes
And the birds are gone, the skies are peaceful,
A cold chill sprays down my freezing spine,
It's getting scary, the streets are deserted
And memories of ghosts fill my twisted mind,
Roasting fires roar in people's houses,
As the fireworks bang in the dark night
And pets are frightened and petrified
And the big Guy Fawkes fire is burning,
The nights are cold as winter creeps near fast,
As the flaky snow hits the cold floor.

Adam James Burrows (11)
St Nicholas RC High School, Hartford

SUMMER

Lying down on the dry grass in the sunlight,
So much better than winter in the cold,
The blue sky now holds a colourful kite,
It's quite hot tomorrow as I am told,
The air is smelling as sweet as honey,
Apples are falling from the bright green trees,
In the distance, I see a white bunny
And the sound of buzzing from the small bees,
It starts to go cloudy, here comes the rain,
Everything turns dark and lights are now on,
All of it patters on the windowpane,
The people playing in the park have gone,
The sun leaves us with cold and dark to come,
Winter draws folk indoors till spring returns.

Dominic Wroblewski (12)
St Nicholas RC High School, Hartford

AUTUMN SONNET

A cold and windy night, all is quiet,
Kids walk round with scary masks on their faces,
It must be Hallowe'en again, but still it's quiet,
Except the rustle of leaves with the wind,
At the start of my day, it's dark and dim,
The sun gets up, there's still a bitter breeze,
The day is dimming, as I walk in the rain,
At night when I sleep, there's a howl of wind,
When Bonfire Night has come
The flames warm my hands,
Catherine wheels shoot fast along a wire,
The fireworks sparkle, smoking as they land,
As the rain comes, it puts out the fire,
The amber remains of the fire glows,
They're floating about as the north wind blows!

Leah Cronin (11)
St Nicholas RC High School, Hartford

ST NICHOLAS SCHOOL RAP

You walk into the classroom, stand up and wait,
Get books out ready, I bet the teacher's late,
Here she comes now, with a smile on her face,
Taking the register at a snail's pace,
Mrs May tells us to get the test tubes out,
Fill them up to the top, when you're finished shout,
Put them on a Bunsen and warm them right up,
When the water starts leaking, you get a cup,
Now it's time to tidy up and pack away,
One more lesson then it's the end of the day.

Jennifer Scott (11)
St Nicholas RC High School, Hartford

Sonnet

Autumn is a great breeze keeping me cool,
Little children hidden behind great masks,
Raindrops splutter on fallen leaves all day,
There aren't any colours left on the trees,
Still autumn has many colours to see,
Golden, crisp leaves blow all around the ground,
Nights are growing longer, days are shorter,
Orangy leaves blow all around the street,
Whilst busy farmers are picking their wheat,
Candlelit pumpkins all down the bright street,
Jumping through the leaves rustling as we play,
The trees look sad, balding, leaves falling fast,
Skies turn from summer blue, now just grey,
Green lush fields start to wither and droop,
Alas the beautiful summer long since past.

Joseph Rimmer (11)
St Nicholas RC High School, Hartford

The Football Stadium

The football stadium,
Holds thousands of people cheering on their team,
Huge, interesting and noisy,
As loud as a rocket shooting off to space,
Holding so many passionate fans,
It makes me feel proud and welcome,
I feel like I belong there,
The football stadium,
It reminds us how much people
Want their team to win.

Gary Scowen (13)
South Wirral High School

My Family

Me dad's like Jim Royle,
Always got a new plan on the boil,
Me mam's like the Queen,
Gives herself airs and graces but
Frankly I think she's mean.

You know those shows on the telly,
Where they film a family - just for fun,
But the family doesn't know - when they
Find out I'll bet they'll be on the run!
The nation laughing at their morning habits,
Watching them running round like mad rabbits.

Well the point of this is -
My family were made for this,
It'd be a show not to miss!
It's like living with a circus,
Except they don't go away.

Me sister thinks she's Britney,
Personally I think she's more of a Whitney,
Me brother's trying to be Slim Shady,
But when he's alone, he dresses like a lady! (Ooh er!)

Sometimes I wonder what that makes me,
But I'd say why don't you just come and see,
It's all a bit strange in our little old pad,
But I wouldn't have it any other way,
It's just a bit mad.

Holly Ostle (15)
South Wirral High School

A Poem Called Monkey!

In swings the chimpanzee,
With his jet-black, silky hair,
His big, brown, baby, button eyes,
Melt me with one stare.

He smiles cheekily on the branches,
He jumps and takes a chance,
Then grabs the climbing rope with his feet
And celebrates with a dance.

He grabs a chunk of apple
And carefully picks out the pips,
He bites into it greedily,
The juice drips down his lips.

He scratches his head in thought
And wonders what to do,
The expression on his face spells mischief,
He swings to the platform to get a better view.

The clown of the jungle sees me
And races through the grass,
He turns and jumps around and tumbles
And presses his face against the glass.

His eyes tell me everything,
He's bored and all alone,
I wonder if he's just realised,
This cage isn't his home . . .

Stuart Gore (15)
South Wirral High School

I Hate Her

Here she comes Miss Perfect,
Her hair tied back in plaits,
All preened and polished with her nails shining,
Sharp and lethal like a cats.

I can feel my eyes watering,
My lips are curling with rage,
My heart flutters in panic,
Like a canary in a cage.

She prances around like she owns the place,
Pouts her lips and flashes that crocodile smile,
I force a grin and she grins back,
But I'm screaming inside all the while.

I swear I could pull out her ice-cold eyes,
That could pierce an apple skin,
I feel my stomach turn and squeeze,
The jealousy is sinking in.

I don't care, do I look bothered?
My intelligence and looks are just fine,
But it's when she walks past I realise,
I'll always be second in line.

But the way she talks makes my blood boil,
I sweat with anger when she speaks,
She's in my English, maths and science,
I've put up with this for weeks.

She swirls a lollipop around her lips,
The boys run down to meet her,
Yes my friend that lolly is sweet,
But revenge is even sweeter . . .

Jannine Sharp (16)
South Wirral High School

Another World

It's hard to imagine just what is under there,
Is it just another world of violence, corruption and war,
Or could it be the perfect world,
We have all longed for?

What do you think is under there?
Perhaps it could be anything you want it to be,
A world full of peace, love and care,
Or perhaps a life full of pollution, violence and war.

I will leave you to decide
What is under there,
Just remember one thing,
It can be anything you want it to be.

Or can it be just our imagination?
Maybe we're all just too hopeful,
For perhaps a perfect world,
Or is it just out of reach?

Peter Todd (14)
South Wirral High School

Colours

Yellow is the colour of sun,
Red is the colour for a heart,
Blue is the colour of ink,
Green is the colour of envy,
Orange is the heart of a fire,
Black is the colour of a dark night,
Multicoloured is the colour of the rainbow.

Lisa Carney (12)
South Wirral High School

When I Am Alone

When I am alone,
I think of many things,
Things I've never thought of before.

When I am alone,
I always remember,
Things that happened last November,
Things I had never done before.

Thoughts like fireworks that light up the sky
And why people lie.

When I am alone,
I think of very strange and magical things,
Thoughts like why is the grass green
And why are people mean?

When I am alone,
I don't know why I think these things
But I do.

Alyson Peterson (14)
South Wirral High School

Writing A Poem

Writing a poem, about anything you say,
I hope it will be finished by the end of the day,
There's so much to write about, so much to do.
I could write about a person, but the question is who?
It's a big wide world, with so much to see,
The world is a lock and I've got the key.

Danielle Durnan (14)
South Wirral High School

The Super Hero

He jumped up high
And flew through the sky,
Doing his usual shift,
(After he said goodbye to his girlfriend,
And giving the postman a lift).

He then saw villains,
Stealing from Dillans,
Taking a thing or two,
(He noticed them cos the shopkeeper was yelling,
'Stop! Now! Yeah you!')

He rocketed down,
Into the town,
To take them to a cop.
(But then he hit a lamp post
And went tumbling into the shop).

He got medical care,
Then flew through the air,
And decided to go back home,
(But first he went to pick up his cheque,
From the super hero dome!)

John Welch (14)
South Wirral High School

War!

Tanks creep and topple forward to the wire,
The barrage roars and lifts, then, clumsily bowed,
With bombs and guns and shovels and battle gear,
Lines of grey and muttering faces masked with fear,
Boom! A nuke, what we had feared the most . . .

Hayden Craill (14)
South Wirral High School

DEATH

Death is coming and you know
There's nowhere to run, nowhere to go,
People are dead, more are dying,
Everyone sees it so they start crying.

Nothing cheers me up anymore, I never give a smile,
Death keeps telling us come on line up, single file,
Will he pick us during the day or in the dark night,
We curl up in a ball afraid with the fright.

I am so hungry, I don't know what to do,
I can feel my ones, see my bones, oh gosh look at you,
Dark appears I am too tired to sleep,
No way can I dream, I will just lie awake and weep.

Lucy Sherratt (13)
South Wirral High School

DIFFERENT

Hello best mates, goodbye Mum,
Hello cinema, goodbye park,
Hello ice pops, goodbye sweets,
Hello mobile phone, goodbye travelling,
Hello texting, goodbye talking,
Hello buses, goodbye walking,
Hello computers, goodbye writing,
Hello spell checker, goodbye dictionary,
Hello new mansions, goodbye old huts,
Hello planners, goodbye scrap paper,
Hello new clothes, goodbye shabby rags.

Becky Church (11)
South Wirral High School

Alone

I'm so alone in the world,
No one wants to comfort me,
Everyone seems to hate me,
Why am I a hated person?

Everyone has someone to talk to -
Apart from me,
I wish I could laugh and mean it,
Instead of crying myself to sleep.

Do you think about your life
And where it's going to?
I think I'll be alone,
All my life and then,
I think of you.

Emma Pritchard (15)
South Wirral High School

Our Top Striker

We're 1-0 up with 10 minutes to go,
Our top striker was on the go.
He skipped past one, skipped past another,
He was even better than my big brother,
He was one-on-one with the 6 foot keeper,
He struck the net in the 90th minute,
The whistle blew, we won 2-0,
We shook hands with the opponents,
To show our respect for one another.

Nik Pollitt (13)
South Wirral High School

MY FAMILY

My mum, my dad, my brother and my sister,
My brother's strange so I call him mister,
I live in a big, four bedroomed house,
I have a cat, a dog but not a mouse,
My nan and my gramps live next door,
I'm always in there, not anymore,
My brother Ste and my sister Charli,
They're always there and drive me barmy,
I walk down the long, cobbly street
And on the way I come to meet,
Carl, Danny, Preston and Paul,
They're in Year 11 and all dead tall,
These are our Ste's mates,
They tell me his secrets about his dates,
So now you know my family
They're sad, mad but cool,
I wouldn't change them for the world,
Because I am not a fool!

Faye Devaney (13)
South Wirral High School

THE CAT

They are a domestic animal,
Fluffy, cute and sweet,
They're as cuddly as cushions
And as soft as a sofa,
Cats make me feel responsible
They make me feel as responsible as a parent,
Cats,
A friendly animal.

Sara Lamb (11)
South Wirral High School

ALONE

What's it like to be alone?
What's it like to be an outsider?
To walk around on your own
And have no one to talk to?
What's it like to see them there,
Talking about you behind your back?
What's it like to be ignored,
To get called names and be hit?
What's it like to have a black eye,
Bruised bones, harmful names left in your head?
What's it like day and night, having no friends,
Just because you do something different?
What's it like to go to the drawer
And take out the medicine box?
What's it like to take the pills,
One after another?
What's it like to be dead?

Lee Taylor (13)
South Wirral High School

THE LIGHTHOUSE

The lighthouse,
Warns the ships of danger in its way,
Sparkly, mighty, large,
Like the sun in the sky,
Like a giant star,
It makes me feel tiny,
Like an ant on the ground.
The lighthouse,
Helps you know where you are.

Sharon Dwyer (11)
South Wirral High School

Betrayed Love

A flower that blossoms in the spring,
A woman who opens the box to her wedding ring.

A star that shines in the sky,
A twinkle in a baby's eye.

Birds that fly, dance and play,
A child that smiles on Christmas Day.

A lion angry in its cage,
A girl that cries in pain and rage.

A ship caught in the treacherous sea,
A sad ending for you and me.

Claire Mackenzie (14)
South Wirral High School

The Storm

The storm is like a raging bull,
That thunders through the sky,
Causing chaos on his way to no-man's-land,
He destroys any object in his way,
The world turns sad and dark,
He takes his rage out on the world,
He wipes the land with darkness
And sadness and cruelty,
He hates the sun.

Kai Winterton (12)
South Wirral High School

FOOTBALL GAME - LIVERPOOL VS EVERTON

'Liverpool, Liverpool!' The crowds all cheer,
Then after the match, they all go for a beer.

Owen to Heskey, Heskey to Gerrard,
Gerrard to Riise, Riise to Cheyrou,
I think reds are better than blues.

Everton, Everton, never score,
Campbell used to but not any more.

Campbell to Ferguson, Ferguson
To Radzinski, Radzinski to Wear,
Wear, Rooney,
He drives me looney.

Erin Rowlands (13)
South Wirral High School

BLACKPOOL LIGHTS

Going down the Golden Mile
Everyone has got a smile,
Bright lights like spaceships,
While everyone is eating bags of chips,
When the trams come around,
They make a horrible sound,
We climb the tower,
It takes us over an hour,
Everyone has got a smile,
Going down the Golden Mile.

Peter Nicholson (13)
South Wirral High School

The Snake

The snake,
The snake has a long dry lethal body,
It's sly, sleek, suspicious,
The snake is like an electric wire,
You never know when it will
Strike!
It's like a small mosquito that no one
Notices until it's struck!
The snake makes me feel nervous and insecure,
The snake,
Remember you're not always alone
When you think you are!

Jack Fawdry (12)
South Wirral High School

My Brother

My younger brother
Born 9 years ago
Strong, tall and cool
Like a steel fighting machine
Like a thousand armies
He makes me feel weak
Like an ant and a human
My younger brother
It reminds me we all need love.

Jade Ashworth (11)
South Wirral High School

THE GIRAFFE

The giraffe,
Has a big neck,
Tall, big, great,
Like a crane in the sky,
Head like a bird, it can see
Over tree tops,
It makes me feel small,
Like a mouse crawling around,
The giraffe,
It reminds me how small I
Really am.

Kimberley Currie (11)
South Wirral High School

DOLPHINS

A dolphin,
Is a mammal,
Big, mighty, cuddly,
Like a huge shark but without the bite,
Like a smooth piece of material,
It makes me feel big,
Like a queen that everyone notices,
A dolphin,
It reminds us how important animals are.

Charlotte Dooley (12)
South Wirral High School

My House

My house,
Where I feel most
Comfortable,
Warm, snug and cosy!
Like the perfect place
Just built for me,
Like it was made for me
To live there,
My house,
Where I feel most
Comfortable.

Leanne O'Brien (11)
South Wirral High School

A Wise Owl

A wise owl
The wisest of all owls
Big, old, glowing,
Like the king of the forest,
Like the wisest of all animals,
It makes me feel dumb,
Like a sheep following a herd of cows,
A wise owl,
It reminds us that we're not as smart as animals.

Thomas Matthews (11)
South Wirral High School

LIVERPOOL!

Liverpool, Liverpool we are the best,
We are better than the rest,
Baros, Baros, he can score goals,
Even more than old Paul Scholes,
Owen, Owen, he's so fast,
He can get past the defence in a blast.
Riise, Riise, he's got a big throw,
He could throw it up to the top row,
Liverpool, Liverpool we are the best,
We are better than the rest.

Andrew Gurney (14)
South Wirral High School

AN ELEPHANT

An elephant,
Lived for years,
Huge, mighty, fat,
Like a great king of the jungle,
Like a hunter with no escape,
It makes me feel small,
Like a bug ready to be crushed,
An elephant,
Reminds us how we think, to do things.

Ashton Taylor (12)
South Wirral High School

My Father

You give to me so much of yourself,
Your time,
Your love,
Your tender care,
That whatever else I may become,
I will be my father's child.
Thanks for teaching me to tie knots,
To fly a kite,
To imagine ships, trains
And secret places I could go,
I could be whatever I wanted to be,
Because you believed in me.

My dad may not be a king,
But he's somewhere in the world
And he may not be rich
But he is wise and good.

And if I had to pick
From all the dads,
In all the world,
The coolest dad of all of them
Would definitely be mine.

Heather Collins (14)
South Wirral High School

Strange Things You See

I saw a can flying in the sky,
I saw a multicoloured fly.

I saw a hundred men kissing the moon,
I saw a butterfly come out of its cocoon.

I saw a hat made out of copper,
I saw a penguin blowing poppers.

I saw a monster which will give you a fright,
I saw a day turn into night.

Danny Evans (11)
South Wirral High School

Caramel And Wispa

I have 2 female rats,
Wispa and Caramel by name,
I find them really funny,
When they're playing games.

They squeak a lot,
Roll around in their bed,
Wispa and Caramel eat anything,
Toast, cheese, I have fed.

They swing in their hammock,
A tube they do run through,
Trying to climb out of their cage,
They find it hard to do.

Now they are nearly 6 months old,
I love them oh so much,
I really like to handle my rats,
My rats are soft to touch.

They love to fight,
They love to eat,
When we're all in bed
Cereal is their treat.

Kate Patterson (11)
South Wirral High School

GRANNY

Hello Granny, are you old?
Lying in that bed,
Your wrinkles are coming
And your bunions are humming.

Hello Granny, are you old?
Lying in that bed,
Your head is getting cold
And your nose is growing mould.

Hello Granny, are you old?
Lying in that bed,
Your eyes are red
And your lips are nearly dead.

Hello Granny, are you old?
Lying in that bed,
Your eyes are red
And your lips are nearly dead.

Kate Fletcher (13)
South Wirral High School

THE SHIMMERING SUN

The shimmering sun
Up so high,
Shining, big, light,
Like a face looking down on us,
Like a burning ball,
It makes me feel hot,
Hotter than a warm day,
The shimmering sun,
We need to use it as light.

Emma Rankin (12)
South Wirral High School

My Poem! Wishes

I wish I had a sis,
I wish I was a great singer,
I wish I had a little puppy,
I hope they all come true.

I wish I had a car,
I wish I had a house,
I wish I had a boyfriend,
I hope they all come true.

I wish there weren't any insects,
I wish there wasn't any rain,
I wish there weren't any dentists,
I hope they all come true.

I wish there weren't any mosquitoes,
I wish there wasn't any school,
I wish there wasn't any fruits,
I hope they all come true.

Rebecca Williams (11)
South Wirral High School

The Budgie

The loud budgie,
Sits on the perch,
Loud, chirps, cheeky,
Colourful as a rainbow,
Bright as a feltip,
Happy on a sunny day,
The loud budgie,
It reminds me how lucky I am.

Kayleigh Worsley (11)
South Wirral High School

CHESS

The soldiers prepare for battle,
Lined up in their attack formation,
They make the first move,
Being cautious, moving one step at a time.
Opening up the back line
And their supreme commander orders them
To charge forward and capture enemies
From the foreign land,
The noblemen and their horses,
Charge over their own troops,
Into the attack run,
The enemies are advancing quickly,
Having wiped out all of their defences,
They are to strong,
The king has surrendered,
The war is over.

Christopher Boardman (14)
South Wirral High School

THE SKYSCRAPER

The skyscraper,
Large and mighty,
Huge, mighty, soaring,
As tall as the Eiffel Tower,
Like a big, fat giant,
Makes me feel like a flea,
The skyscraper,
Bigger than big can be.

Jack Eccleston (11)
South Wirral High School

Cats' Eyes

Cats aren't just domestic animals,
They are big as well.
The kind of cat I'm talking about
Is a dangerous, man-eating one.
The eyes, if you look deep into the eyes,
Of this beautiful creature you can see,
Its true feelings, it is scared, lonely
And in danger.

Look into the eyes of this beautiful creature
And you can see fear of man,
Think,
If you were this creature,
You'd be scared,
Think,
When you buy a fur scarf or coat,
Think,
Of what creature you're buying and killing.

Bethany MacDougall (11)
South Wirral High School

The Black Panther

The black panther,
Leopard of the night,
Sly, deadly and swift,
Like fire, pretty but fierce,
Like a ghost of the jungle,
Watching, waiting by the moonlight,
The black panther,
Discover the mysteries around you.

Kerris McKinlay Whyte (11)
South Wirral High School

Money

Money, money everywhere
And all you want to spend,
However, everyone can stand to spare
A little cash to lend,
To send a few bucks to a
Friend in need,
But if you don't give a dime,
You will hear your death bells chime.

If you give a dollar then
In the end you will hear
Wedding bells ring.
You may be poor but happy
And pleased with no need with money.

Brian Hill (13)
South Wirral High School

Life

Life does not last forever,
Short, precious, amazing,
Like space it will go on but different,
Every step,
Like colour it fades,
Makes me feel insignificant,
Like a single grain of sand,
Life,
You think now and why.

Naomi Russell-Baugh (12)
South Wirral High School

Buildings, Buildings

Buildings, buildings, way up high,
Will they still be there when I die?
Bigger than trees, just poking through the sky,
Buildings, buildings, way up there.
Bigger than mountains, as strong as a bear,
Made out of bricks, brown as sticks,
Just standing there, without a care.
September the 11th,
What a tragedy,
Who would do such a thing?
Not you or me.
Rubble, wreckage everywhere,
In our clothes and in our hair,
Many lives taken because of one man,
He only did it, because he can.

Christopher Russell (12)
South Wirral High School

Changes

Hello new house mates, goodbye Mum,
Hello work, goodbye school,
Hello spots, goodbye chocolate,
Hello new brick houses, goodbye wooden huts,
Hello cars, goodbye walking,
Hello texting, goodbye conversation,
Hello Internet, goodbye books,
Hello clocks, goodbye hourglass,
Hello designer labels, goodbye rags,
Hello free choice, goodbye slavery.

Nikki Hanmer (11)
South Wirral High School

The Frog

The frog lives in swamps, rivers and streams,
It has a brother, the toad and it's very cold,
The frog is green like a bean,
It's very small just bigger than a bouncy ball.

It has a long tongue for catching flies,
Because a frog never dies,
It can't read, it can't write,
But it can fight.

It can't walk, it has to hop,
Then it drops,
They are excellent swimmers,
Better than us,
I bet they are not allowed on the bus,
Goodbye.

Thanks Mr Frog.

Nathan Tripp (11)
South Wirral High School

The Rabbit

Pointy ears,
Hops around,
Likes to burrow in the ground,
He's like a cute, fluffy teddy bear,
He's like a mad bull charging around,
You can stroke him all the time,
To keep him locked up is such a crime,
What a lovely pet, he's not even one yet.

Lisa Reynolds (11)
South Wirral High School

Silent Snow

The blanket of snow lay still across the floor,
Spread around the windows and all over the door,
The first footprints sink deep as they go,
They lie there everywhere, all over the snow.

The snowballs fly right through the air,
Children are throwing them everywhere,
The snow lies still on top of the trees,
All over the branches and all over the leaves.

The snow melts later on into the day,
Everyone's wishing it was here to stay,
It melts and melts, till there's nothing there to show,
Now everyone's waiting till the next winter's snow!

Alicia Gleeson (12)
South Wirral High School

The Moon

When I look out of my window at night,
All I see gives me a fright,
The wind howls
And dogs growl,
Evil things crawl around,
Smiling at me upon the ground,
But then I look up at the sky,
I see the moon shining down from up high,
I smile back climbing into bed,
As my trusty night light
Shines down on me.

Lloyd Greenall (12)
South Wirral High School

SISTERS

Me and my sister fight like cats,
We fight about this and we fight about that,
My mum always says, 'Just leave her alone.'
'But she's winding me up,' I always moan.
'Why don't you make up and give her a hug?'
'But yesterday, Mum, she broke my mug!'
'Okay, okay,' I agree,
My sister looks up and laughs at me.
'Why would I want to be friends with you?
I'd prefer to be friends with a monkey from a zoo.'
'Can I borrow your feathery clip?
It's the only one matching this outfit.'
'Alright, you can have it on loan,
But don't think you're keeping it,' comes the groan.
'Well can I use your Puma bag?
Pretty please or I will nag.'
Mum comes in and says, 'What's going on?'
'Danielle's got sweets and won't give me one.'
'Go away and play with your friends!
Let's put this argument to an end!'

Danielle Smith (12)
South Wirral High School

WISH POEMS

I wish I was a superstar,
I wish I was so rich,
I wish I was a great singer
And I wish my wishes came true.

I wish there were no vegetables,
I wish there was no mist,
I wish there wasn't mosquitoes
And I wish my wishes came true.

I wish I had a PlayStation 2
I wish I had a puppy,
I wish I had a baby sister
And I wish my wishes came true.

Lyndsey Lloyd (12)
South Wirral High School

ADJECTIVES

Rapidly, a cheetah runs for its prey,
Rapidly, the children come out to play,
Rapidly, a pencil turns blunt,
Rapidly, an owl wakes up to hunt,
Rapidly, a pigeon flies down for some bread,
Rapidly, a headache comes up to my head,
Rapidly, the time turns on the clock,
Rapidly, I put on my party frock,
Rapidly, the last dance is over,
Rapidly, I fall asleep and turn over.

Slowly, a snail crosses the road,
Slowly, tadpoles turn into toads,
Slowly, a sheep chomps the grass,
Slowly, a cloth reaches the glass,
Slowly, Christmas time approaches,
Slowly, I wait for holiday coaches,
Slowly, the turtle reaches the shore,
Slowly, the rich turns to poor,
Slowly, poorness turns to hunger,
Slowly, time passes but I'll never get any younger.

Katrina Taylor (11)
South Wirral High School

SNOW

Snow falls from the sky in flakes
As it hits the ground it breaks,
It is very cold and white
When it falls on you it feels so light!

Snow is hard when rolled in a ball
That's why snowmen never fall,
With their big round heads
They are still, they can't move
Really they are dead!

Snow is cold it freezes your hands
It's not like a beach where it's hot
And has sand.
Snow is great, it makes me feel happy
If it gets on you it makes you feel soggy!

Penny Hassall (12)
South Wirral High School

THE CROCODILE!

The crocodile,
Slowly slithering through the murky
Waters of Africa, sliding, creeping,
Swimming, searching for its prey.
Silently like a snake in the desert
Scaly skin, unblinking eyes,
A great big grin of sparkly, white teeth,
Relaxing in the river soaking in the sun
Suddenly . . .
Snap!

Hannah Brown (11)
South Wirral High School

The Sun

On a hot day I look way up high
And wonder who threw the sun up in the sky,
Where, oh where does it go at night,
When the moon and stars are shining bright?

As yellow as the sand,
As round as a beach ball,
It burns up there,
Will it ever fall?

At dawn the sun will rise,
As the farmers cockerel suddenly cries,
All my thoughts turned into one,
A big ball of fire we all call the sun.

Katie Spiller (13)
South Wirral High School

Ducks

Ducks are cute and cuddly too,
Well I think they are so,
How about you?
Some are yellow and some are brown,
Some are green
And sometimes never to be seen.
They usually bob up and down
And sometimes look like a funny clown,
Ducks are cute and cuddly too,
Well I think they are so,
How about you?

Emma Harris (13)
South Wirral High School

Computer Game

All I was doing was
Playing the game.

When the computer
Froze, it was a computer shame.

I was standing
When lightning struck.

It frightened me a lot,
I wasn't having much luck.

Just as I was about to pack away,
Something came out and wanted to play.

Jamie Leeke (12)
South Wirral High School

What Is What?

Red is violence,
Black is death,
Blue is Heaven,
White is music,
Green is nature,
Purple is violets,
Orange is Hell,
Pink is a girlfriend,
Yellow is sunlight,
Brown is a branch,
Silver is moonlight,
Gold is pirate's treasure,
Platinum is a milk bottle top.

Michael Gartland (11)
South Wirral High School

FRIENDS

They are always there,
Whenever you are down,
Whenever you get a scare,
They are always around.
If I fall over,
Graze my knee,
They rush over
And rescue me.
I wish they lived at home,
To play on the PlayStation
And talk on the phone.
Even if we break up now,
I will still love them somehow.
At the end of the day,
I have to say goodbye,
I will always say okay,
But still I sigh.

Amanda Fewtrell (12)
South Wirral High School

THE HEDGEHOG

The hedgehog,
Small and prickly,
Brown, sharp, spiky,
Like a ball of pins,
A nose like a button,
Making me feel happy,
Like a lamb taking its first leap,
The hedgehog,
Reminds me of winter.

Kim Hullock (11)
South Wirral High School

I Saw

I saw a dog singing
I saw two birds drinking
I saw a man flying
I saw a mouse crying
I saw girl barking
I saw a car parking

I saw a snake with legs
I saw a lion with two heads
I saw a monkey made out of lead
I saw a Hoover lying in bed

These may sound like they're from my imagination
But they're just God's creation.

Amy Evans (12)
South Wirral High School

Mum

My mum is good
My mum makes me pud,
She makes me tea.

My mum puts me in bed
And she kisses my head,
She gets me up in the morning
And she says, 'Crack of dawning.'

My mum makes me breakfast
And says I am hopeless,
Because I am dopey.

Daniel Kinsley-Smith (12)
South Wirral High School

I Am The Boy

I am the boy that you see every day
I am the boy that runs away
I am the boy who only wants to play

I am the boy!

I am the boy that is quite dumb
I am the boy that loves his mum
I am the boy who looks very glum

I am the boy!

I am the boy who is quite sad
I am the boy who loves his dad
I am the boy who is very mad

I am the boy!

Michael Oliver (12)
South Wirral High School

What Is He?

The day he came, he stole my heart,
His tiny toes, they broke my heart,
He did not do anything but sleep,
He must have been counting too many sheep
Even though he sleeps, sleeps, sleeps,
His tiny mouth and tiny feet, I will not forget,
So can you guess what he is?
His name is
Milo, so have a guess . . .

Yasmin Combe
South Wirral High School

My Little Bunny

My little bunny hops,
My little bunny springs,
My little bunny runs around,
My little bunny jumps like he has wings.

My little bunny is cuddly,
My little bunny is round,
My little bunny is furry,
My little bunny is so big it bounces on the ground.

My little bunny is there when I'm happy,
My little bunny is there when I'm sad,
My little bunny is there even when I'm bad
And I'm there for my little bunny
When he needs a cuddle at night.

Sundus Ahmad (12)
The Kingsway School

Stick Men

What is wrong with stick men?
They used to be in fashion,
But now the stick men trade,
Oh the stick men trade's a-crashin'.
The people that you draw today
Have clothes and face expressions,
But oh the poor old stick men,
They're suffering from depression.
So bear a thought when drawing men
And make sure that they don't look too vain,
Cos if you just stop drawing them
There won't be any more of those
Stick men.

Hannah Dickinson (13)
The Kingsway School

HOLLY

The milkman doesn't mind her,
The bin men really like her,
The mailman can't quite stand her,
This is about Holly!

There is a little dog called Holly,
Who is really rather jolly,
She lives not very far from me
And out of the window she can see:

People passing the house,
Thinks she's as quiet as a mouse,
But little do they know,
What's about to show.

She wags her tail at me,
I wave at her and say,
'Hello Holly,
How are you today?'

The owners also have a cat,
But I'm not very fond of that,
They stare and stare all through the day,
Until it's time for them to play!

If only Holly could talk,
She'd ask me for a walk,
I'd take her every day,
Even when I'm out at play!

The milkman doesn't mind her,
The bin men really like her,
The mailman can't quite stand her,
That's about Holly!

Melissa Thurrell (11)
The Kingsway School

A Poem To Faith On Her Christening

Don't judge a person by their features,
Love and care for all God's creatures.

Remember manners and never stare,
Help your elders and give up your chair.

Sometimes stop and wait a while,
See sad faces but give a smile.

Cheer people up don't feel blue,
Succeed and try in all you do.

Tell younger people all you know,
Listen and learn as you grow.

The most horrible thing in this world is war,
There's meant to be peace but others want more.

When you were born your hair was black as night,
Whenever I see you I want to hug you tight!

Katie Victoria Hudghton (11)
The Kingsway School

Kingsway

Lots of different people,
Lots of new faces,
People who are Asian
And lots more different races.

People from quite far away
And some that live next door,
It doesn't matter where you're from
Or what you look like at all.

Kingsway is a huge school, much bigger
Than the rest
And when it comes to competition,
Then Kingsway are the best!

You have lots of fun
And make loads of new friends,
When you're in a school as good as this,
Your laughter never ends!

Joshua Bull (11)
The Kingsway School

PRECIOUS THE BUNNY

Precious is a lovely bunny
She is really rather funny
She belongs to my friend
Fluffy, cute, cuddly
That's Precious alright.

In and out of the cage
That's how Precious spends her days
Munching, crunching away on her food
Not a care in the world, a life to choose
That's Precious alright.

Playful, friendly, all the while,
The whole garden is her playground,
To her, her time is worthwhile.
The life of a rabbit it would do for me!
That's Precious alright!

Emily Gillison (11)
The Kingsway School

SCHOOL

School is getting up too early
School is graffiti in books

School is squeaky chalk on the blackboards
School is muddy shoes on a clean floor

School is screaming kids
School is too much homework . . . way too much

School is the smell of chips from the canteen
School is the annoying tick-tock of clocks

School is being pushed in the playground
School is being teased about new haircuts

School is a boring detention
School is certificates in assembly

School is losing your dinner money
School is cheering when the rattling bell rings.

Alice Dickinson (12)
The Kingsway School

PANDA PANDEMONIUM

Pandas shuffling,
Pandas snuffling,
Pandas finding new bamboo,
Pandas hiding from me and you.
It's panda pandemonium!
Pandas keeping their coats intact,
I know it sounds strange but it's a fact,
For it's panda pandemonium!

Ruth Emery (11)
The Kingsway School

Little People

All the little people in their tree house,
about the size of a tiny, little mouse.
All the little people hovering in the sky,
with their delicate wings that enable them to fly.

Hiding in the bushes so as not to be seen,
with the pretty flowers and the leaves so green.
Singing very sweetly they hardly make a sound,
even looking closely you won't see them around.

Doing fairy magic from morning to the night,
but sights and sounds of big people gives them such a fright.
They cannot be seen by the likes of you or I,
only by special people like through a child's eye.

Megan Humphreys (12)
The Kingsway School

Yellow

Yellow is the colour of the sunshine,
Glistening on waters, turning them gold.
Yellow makes you feel happy,
But sticky and hot.
Yellow is the colour of citrus fruits,
Lemons and melons.
Yellow is the sand beneath your feet,
On the hot, sandy beach.
Yellow makes the sunshine blinding,
Giving you the chance to wear your
New shades.

Parisã Haghighi (13)
The Queen's School

School Dinners

As I enter the dinner hall,
all the tables and chairs stand to attention,
like an army on inspection parade.
The queue is as long as a python
hissing for its food angrily.
The dinner ladies always stand
behind the table with a beam
on their face as wide as the ocean's floor.
As I wait I can smell the hot puddings.
They smell like a garden
on a summer's day
and I can't wait to explore!
On the counter I can see
a contrast of colours,
greens, yellows, reds, purples and pinks,
joining together like a rainbow.
The pizza is like a map of the world,
coated in a thick layer of cheese.
For pudding there is a large selection.
The jelly looks like a drunken man,
but as colourful as a butterfly.
I think I might have that.
On the other side there is chocolate cake,
my best friend will be pleased!
It looks like a huge mound of thick, slimy mud,
but tasty all the same!
Finally I start to eat my tasty, but interesting
school dinner!

Jacklyn Smith (12)
The Queen's School

My Special Place

I dug my fingers into a crevice in the rock,
The roar of the waterfall,
Deafening me,
The water,
Hitting the plunge pool below,
Crystal drops of spray flecked my face,
Hazy mists hung around the waterfall,
A faint halo,
I heaved myself up into the cave,
Golden sand carpeted the floor,
Softening the jagged rocks underneath,
A glassy sheet covered the mouth of the cave,
Little streams trickled down the craggy walls,
Forming pools in the sand,
Green and brown blurs smudged the clear glass,
The powerful forest,
Not wanting to be forgotten by me,
I outstretched my warm hand,
Plunging it through the water,
The force pushed me down and down,
My hand,
Interrupting its straight course,
The water stung me,
Gnawing like a thousand sharks' teeth in a vast,
Sparkling ocean,
The pain,
Unbearable,
I withdrew my hand,
Nobody knows about my special place,
Just me and the waterfall.

Helen Gaster (12)
The Queen's School

The Dolphin

Gliding softly, silently through the sea,
A bird in the sky,
Water rushes past her like a breeze,
Coral reefs of brilliant reds,
Oranges and yellows beneath her.
Tropical fish dart in-between rocks like arrows,
Her silvery skin shines and glints,
Soft and rubbery,
Warm and smooth to the touch.
Gracefully floating,
Navigating that crystal clear sea,
Her eyes are bright, beady, black,
A stunning, magnificent creature is she,
She travels in the rays of the sun,
That catch her eye, glinting.
Scared, she slows down,
Ignoring the craving curiosity, she swims on,
Fear seems to leak away,
She glides softly to the surface,
Closer, closer . . .
To the break
Between wet water and dry air,
Gathering up speed . . .
She leaps up into the air,
Like a lion onto its prey,
Wind whistles past her slim body,
Up here the ocean is a gorgeous gold.
Splash!
The elegant, silvery-grey body hits the water
And quickly dives into the deep.

Natalia Caldecott (11)
The Queen's School

HENRY VIII: WIFE NUMBER SIX

Henry VIII sat on his throne
You should have heard him moan and groan:
'I'm getting fat and dull and old,
I've lost some hair; I'm going bald.
I feel that I am drained and lifeless,
And to cap it off I'm broke and wifeless!'
With that he slumped back down like jelly
Lost beneath his folds of belly.
His courtiers raised their brows and sighed,
You really think they should have lied.
But no, they did not dare refuse
They fetched the king a can of booze.
'You rest now Sir, here's what we'll do,
Please forget wife number two
And do away with three and four,
Admit wife five was such a bore,
Trust us now, we'll find a fix
A charming, good wife number six!'
They chanced upon young Katherine Parr,
All Henry's friends went, 'Ooh!' and 'Ahh!'
The king proposed right there and then,
Next day they married: Katherine to Hen.
Two years on, Henry's health went bad,
When put on a diet he went raving mad.
Soon after that, King Hen was dead
'It wasn't the carrot,' the chief cook said.
The funeral was sad and weepy,
Although the priest was rather sleepy.
A week after her husband died,
Kath was praised cos she survived!

Sing Yun Lee (12)
The Queen's School

SUCH IS THE NATURE OF THE ISLAND

Diamond fragments reflect
Off the pure sand,
Like the preserved carpet of a majestic room,
Without trace of life, it lies -
Undisturbed.

Beyond the carpet, lying in stateliness,
Is a deep azure haven, in which
White galloping horses race with the tide,
And roll into the palm-ridden shore -
Thundering.

The brilliant waters penetrate the island.
Silver lakes and crystal streams
Trickle through the emerald-green climbers
And the mangroves -
Tropical.

The glittered sky of sunbeams in the day
And of the stars in the night,
Shines over the vast stretch of beach
And the unclouded sun smiles,
Giving warmth.

The exotic plants give
Fresh, ripe fruit and heavenly blossoms scent
The jungle surroundings, the exquisite perfume
Carried by the gentle onshore breeze -
Refreshing.

Rising mists of heat from the baking sand,
Images, mirages entice a wandering visitor,
To be or not to be? That is the question.
A cooling drink or just a reflection?
Trickery.

Nicki-Jayne Russell (13)
The Queen's School

Ageing Seasons

'Cab, sir?'
You smile as he shakes his head
And stare into the sky.
Grey now, cloaked with the stationary deep silver-blue clouds
As a last, unsolved care
Like the aged, weary, cynical air
Of your customer

'Cab, sir?'
You smile as he shakes his head
And stare into the sky.
White now, and not hidden by the empty clouds of before
As a child's first nameless fear
Like the snowdrop, the first flower of a new year
That flowers in the cold

'Cab, sir?'
You smile as he shakes his head
And stare into the sky.
Blue now, with white bunny-tail clouds that fly across randomly
As a wisp of a dream
Like the white-as-moonlight new milk, frothed with cream
Drunk for strength

'Cab, sir?'
You smile as he shakes his head
And stare into the sky.
Wise now, the white new-chick clouds silver with seeing
As a story told
Like a claw, the knife that tears between new and old
Golden sharp
'No, thank you.'

Harriet Houlsby (13)
The Queen's School

SEA BREEZE

This desert island,
Once so full of life,
With songs of birds in the trees,
Was suddenly turned into Satan's lair.
On that night,
That dreaded night,
When the wind swept in from the seas.

A perfect day it had been,
As good as any one,
With the constant sound of buzzing bees.
Then, came a deep rumble from above.
On that night,
That dreaded night,
When the wind swept in from the seas.

A whistling was heard,
A chill was felt,
The grass was now grey and not so green
And a dark carpet swept over the sky.
On that night,
That dreaded night,
When the wind swept in from the seas.

Now it's silent.
Everything is so bare.
I'm all alone, no one here but me.
I'm giving up. I'll be here forever.
Because of that night,
That final night,
When the wind swept in from the seas.

Georgia Whiteoak (13)
The Queen's School

A War Poem

The air raid siren screaming
And searchlights brightly gleaming,
Terror! Terror!

Shot out of my sleep,
Deafened by the noise,
Down the narrow stairs I creep,
Sobbing for my mother.

Onto the street I run,
Pushing through the crowds,
What have the Nazis done?
Why take so many lives?

A thousand thoughts running through my head,
A thousand colours in the sky,
Why should I walk on the path of life,
While those around me die?

Stumbling down some steps,
Half pushed by those behind me,
Water trickling down the walls,
So many faces I don't know - where is she?

Safe now, but for how long?
Nearly killed but have done no wrong,
Oh, why should my life coincide
With World War and genocide?

The air raid siren screaming
And searchlights brightly gleaming,
Terror! Terror!

Emily Tooke (11)
The Queen's School

The Island Isn't All That It Seems

The white, golden sand glistens,
The birds squawk in the palms,
The sun sends out its warm rays,
The sea breeze is calming.

The azure brine flows free,
Like a shimmering snake,
It moves on rhythmically
And on the shore it splashes.

Refreshing water sparkles,
Like deep blue diamonds shine.
The soft, salty aroma,
Is wafted in the wind.

The sun's warm rays seem friendly,
But they cause suffering.
Strange creatures lurk in the dark,
Waiting for their next kill.

The paradise's beauty,
Hides its true wickedness.
Its dark, unfriendly shadows,
Its pain inflicting heat.

Louise Stride (13)
The Queen's School

Voices

Voices in a crowded room
Like the rise and fall of an orchestra.
Piping, like a flute
Low, like rumbling drums
Drifting around.
Wheedling, like sickly, sweet honey
Oozing from a honeycomb.

Angry, like snarling dogs
Fighting over a bone
As if their life depended on it.
Irritating like a dripping tap
That can't be switched off.
Like a trembling jelly,
Like a monotonous drone,
Like an excited crescendo.

Alison Wheatland (12)
The Queen's School

World War II

Constant shuddering,
Earth and soil trickles
from the roof of the shelter.

Moaning Minnie
wails again,
Warning of the German bombers.

People quiver and shout,
Run and run
forever.

'Shelter here,' people cry,
Not long before the
engine cuts out above.

People and houses
fall,
Crippled and dead.

The war is on.

Hannah Donald (12)
The Queen's School

The Hermit

He sits alone with a content look on his face,
No worries or problems ruin his deep thoughts.

His shaggy mane blows in the icy autumn breeze,
The holes in his derelict coat are filled with emotions
And feelings.
His rosy cheeks are like glossy, newly picked apples.
His expression is solemn.

The sharp, blue waves lick his battered, ill feet.
The sand washes over his body.
His grey eyes pierce the brick-like horizon,
Setting into the late evening sun.

The flying, golden sand surrounds him and his vision is cut.
He is blind.
Crabs scuttle nearby as the gulls screech.
The season changes as rain trickles down his
Happy appearance.

He stands alone with an anxious look on his face,
The season has ruined his deep thoughts.

Nicola Pether (12)
The Queen's School

Him

His clothes are dirty, smelly and torn,
He always looks depressingly forlorn.
To see this young man as a moneyless tramp,
Upsets me to think he is in the cold and damp.

To become a drug addict destroys people's lives,
The tramp on the street gives out terrible cries.
Whether it's heroin, cocaine or even ecstasy,
It will ruin the lives of you and me.

He begs on the street for drug money,
But some people think it is funny.
He only ever gets the odd penny,
But I suppose it is the same for many.

Now today he is no longer a tramp
And he does not sit outside in the cold and the damp.
Sadly he has disappeared and it is all because of drugs,
Now he is only a distant memory of a tramp grasping a mug.

Charlotte Mather (14)
The Queen's School

WOODLAND WONDERLAND

The watery sun shines through the autumn leaves,
As I walk in my wonderland,
The chirp of a bird echoes serenely throughout the branches.
My mind begins to wander and then, I am away,
The daydream taking over.
Can this be real?
I do not know.
The beauty of this place is overwhelming.
The thought continues to prosper in my mind.
The bowing branches sway, their delicate leaves, dying.
Frail and helpless, they fall to the ground.
They resemble parachutes
Gliding,
gliding.
Conkers scatter the leafy ground.
The sun has gone now, night is drawing in on us.
I leave the wood, my haven.
Back to the real world.

Charlotte Meara (11)
The Queen's School

BLACK

A screen, a shutter, a curtain, a blind,
used to shut out light, leave black behind.
A corner, a cupboard, a shadowed side,
all the places where black will hide.
An elegant script written on a page,
used to express feelings of sadness and rage.

Black is that of the night sky,
the blackened corners where owls fly,
the black of shadow where bats squeak high.

The black of mourning,
never boring.

All is black,
Never light.
All is black,
The black of night.

Stephanie Kynaston (12)
The Queen's School

THE DRAWING ROOM

I knelt on the grass,
My purple shirt flowed around me,
The golden, crisp grass swayed,
The sky above me swirled,
I lay below the midnight sky.

I was awoken by the bang of the sky,
I jumped up and leapt in the direction of my house,
The wind whipped my face,
As I ran as fast as I could.

I was now in the comfort of the drawing room,
My red jumper lying on the wicker chair,
Gaecia the cat purred softly in the corner of the room,
The table was lit by the moonlight,
Whilst the stars smiled happily to themselves.

Emma Shore (12)
The Queen's School

A Bird's Eye View

As I look down on England,
What do I see?
I see hell break loose,
On a killing spree.

How quickly the bombs fall,
Destroying London town,
Damaging the houses,
Bringing them down.

Fire's a-raging,
On the ground below,
People are running,
With nowhere to go.

My plane is diving down,
Diving to meet the glow,
I am after a target,
A target that will not go.

I must stop this war,
All this death, all this pain,
Please, oh god of war,
Let it never come again.

Libby Anderson (11)
The Queen's School

THE GREAT SKY BATTLE

Sun bursts out
An horrific beam of light,
Charging through
Bedridden clouds,
To reach the enterprise
Of ruling sky.
Cloud fights back,
Dissolving absorbent sun
Into a mass of darkness.
All light seems to be lost,
For eternity.
Sun is mad,
He scrutinises cloud,
Menacingly, great harm
And intention meant.
Cloud suddenly
Retaliates,
Torturing sun,
Raining unnecessarily,
On top of him,
They will not and
Cannot grant their peace.

Catherine Sarah Barnard (11)
The Queen's School

RESTLESS MIND

I wept all that night
Down, down, down, drowning in turmoil and despair
Goblins of paranoia dissolving the last threads of sanity
I yearn for dreamless sleep

Block the overwhelming misery that penetrates my mind
But sleep, never have you been so elusive.
A frantic search for answers that just can't be found
Please tell me why - and silence a wretched mind.

Laura Brown (12)
The Queen's School

BECKY

Born long before me,
Herself the baby of the family
She accepted my arrival
With sweetness and love,
Licking my tiny hands
Raising an ear to my
Odd, infant noises.

I grew up with her,
A cuddly, white, bouncing ball of fur
Forever playful, always eager
To pack life with fun.
She was my gentle pal.
Always there for me
When life became too tough.

Last week she left me,
Gave up the struggle to draw each breath,
Looked up at me with soulful eyes
And said her last goodbyes.
We buried her under the elm,
Where we can feel her
Sweet, loving presence.

Alexandra Kinsey (11)
The Queen's School

TRAFFIC QUEUE

Off we go in a rush,
We make our space in the traffic and wait to the pushed,
Like a game for two,
We then wait for our metre of space
And if we don't move we get a puzzled face,
Like a jigsaw which is impossible to solve,
We then concentrate on the other car
And ask the driver if it's far.
Then we start to move and we go past a couple of straws
And then we stop and everyone gets sad
And the driver gets mad,
Then an unending sound hits the air
And a red and white flash goes past,
Which is going awfully fast.
At that moment everyone goes blank,
Then someone forgets something
And to liven us up someone sings,
Then at the end of the line two machines are beaten up.
We then go to take a break
Until we awake.

Gail Newland (12)
The Queen's School

CHARLOTTE'S CONDITION

Charlotte sits in her chair and reads,
    She longs to be out with other girls of her age,
    She wants to dance, skip and run,
    But Charlotte knows she can't.

Charlotte's condition is incurable,
    She knows her life will never be quite right,
    She will always be different from everyone else,
    But Charlotte is still strong, she must remain strong.

Sat in her chair, Charlotte could cry,
She could break down and be miserable,
But Charlotte knows it would achieve nothing,
So she lives her life as well as she can.

Eleanor Hulme (12)
The Queen's School

IMPULSIVE

The sky is a child's attempt,
Just shattering, impulsive blue.
The artist would have tones, textures, shadings,
Wrong, the sky is
Just shattering, impulsive blue.

It cheers the sand, without it a dull, lifeless debris,
It coaxes the rebellious sea,
To change its attitude and become the maker of dreams.
It is the king who proudly holds his sceptre,
The sceptre that will bring life and beauty to his people.

Yet although the king and his sceptre can cheer the island -
I am too lonely.
At first the sun kissing my delicate skin
Gave me hope that I would be rescued.
But now the scraping on my blistered skin
Makes my soul cry out with suffocation.

My soul has left me to find other souls on the island,
Souls to communicate with, to reassure me I am still alive.
But all it has found is what oppresses me the most,
The sky,
Just shattering, impulsive blue.

Sarah Warburton (13)
The Queen's School

All The Colours

B lue is the heart of some colours.
L ook at the sky, you see blue on a clear day.
U sed for the colour of the sea.
E very shade of blue is soothing for me.

Y ou think of fruit, lemons and melons.
E ven the sun is yellow.
L ight is drawn as yellow streaks,
L eading the way.
O ur world would be dull and boring
W ithout it.

R emembrance Sunday and poppies red.
E veryone has red with them, it's the key of life
D eep love.

Helen Skupski (12)
The Queen's School

A German

A German,
Walking stately and tall,
Why is he going
to bomb us all?
We're frightened,
We're sick with devastation,
There is fighting and killing
all over the nation.
It's difficult to describe
how terrified I am;
Just waiting in this
White Nazi van.

Rachael Lindsay (11)
The Queen's School

WINTER IS HERE

The crisp leaves crunch under my feet
They glisten in the sunlight
Like precious jewels
With a light coat of ice on them
The trees look bare and unwanted
Every so often when the wind blows
The trees sway
And the leaves rustle about and dance in the wind
It sounds like the cheers from a football ground
Then . . .

Silence.

The towering shadows of the trees
Look like motionless figures.
Winter is here.

Hannah Baker (12)
The Queen's School

THE SEA

It ripples, waving
Like a bird flying calmly through the air.
The surface
Like a delicate layer of crystals,
Lapping over each other.
Deep down the blue turns to black.
Day into night
The world is dark
Back into day,
They greet me with a smile
And
Silence.

Elizabeth Jones (13)
The Queen's School

THE ISLAND

On my island,
A place that only I can go,
There is sand,
Of moonlight glow.

On my island,
Oberon and Titania dance,
Just above land,
Where Bottom sleeps in a trance.

On my island,
Beneath the sun's trapped golden rays,
Sleeps a Psammead or fairy of the sand
And from the ashes a phoenix is raised.

On my island,
Dragons lurk,
Though I dream, on land . . .
'Right! Read page 23 for homework.'

Katherine Brown (13)
The Queen's School

BEACH WATCH

I take cover under a stripy shade
and watch the happy children play.
They kick the waves to make a splash,
wet T-shirts stretched against the sun's rays.

I see men watch the parade of girls,
I hear the tap, tap of ball to bat.
I see the boats far away not seeming to move
and the old men wearing ridiculous hats.

I see timid crabs peep out of their holes
and frothy waves dancing onto the sand.
I see loving couples gently smoothing in cream
and toddlers wearing ice cream on face and on hands.

Sophie Roberts (12)
The Queen's School

THE LOST TRAVELLER

The traveller dismounted his sturdy raft,
Broken by rocks to a size near half.
He made his way to the welcome land
And ran his gnarled fingers through the silken sand.

Strong, rich aromas of spice filled the air,
A product of wind and the sun's fierce glare.
The trees stood stately, tall and lean,
Their swollen leaves a foreign green.

The weary young man felt the island quite massive,
Restrained by the azure, obstructing its passage.
The sun fell low, descending the sky,
Making way for the moon's reign on high.

Sufficiently rested and homeward-bound,
He shook his torn cloak and turned slowly around.
The sight, which met him, was not one of glee,
But his faithful old raft drifting out to the sea.

Emily Meara (13)
The Queen's School

A World Of Its Own

The island is like a crown set in the silver sea,
Every inch of land is a different jewel.

The jungle - the heart of the little paradise;
Palm trees appear like metal to a magnet;
Monkeys swing as though they are made of elastic,
Going one way and then the other;
Parrots squawk, tigers roar, an elephant trumpets.
This little paradise is never still.

The beach - a barrier around the island.
Sand is a carpet of grains,
The colour of the sun.
Shells appear randomly, the shape of horns,
All the colours of the rainbow,
The texture of daggers and yet still soft.

The sea - a world of its own,
The crystal clear water,
Looks as if a dive would break it in half.
The fish are like stars in the sky;
The waves are so calm and gentle,
Lapping in and out, trying to hypnotise you.

Everything on this sleepy island is peaceful,
Hoping it will stay like this.

Rebecca Howlett (13)
The Queen's School

Paradise?

The untouched grains of sand,
Glisten in the sun.
The water gently strokes the island side.
But there's no one here,
No one to find you,
Even if you cried and cried.

In the gentle breeze,
The palm trees sway,
Like feathers, obeying the wind.
But behind the trees,
Lurks evil, punishing you,
Even if you haven't sinned.

In the heavenly sun,
The ocean sparkles,
No longer water but diamonds and pearls.
But in these depths,
Lives have been lost,
Men and women, boys and girls.

This beauty of the earth,
This angel's playground,
It's your special place never to be known.
But then, you will see,
This paradise is nothing,
For even life has no worth when you're alone.

Olly Famoriyo (13)
The Queen's School

TIME TRAVELLER

Singing like an old pit canary,
Always about his childhood,
He swooped into the room,
His face scarred, his voice cracked,
His eyes darting, left, right, left, right.

His smile shone of his pit days,
Of when he mined all day through,
His eyes were wide, like a bird's egg,
Like those from when he went nesting.

But I was glad of his presence,
Glad that he had lived to tell his tales,
Only through him could I travel through time,
Visit the past, abandon the future.

His clothes were old, tattered and worn,
He wore them day in, day out,
He knew nothing but the wilderness of Stoneygate,
His home, his life.

Through his eyes I could relive the past,
See the darkness all around,
Smell the flames of the flickering lamps,
Feel the emptiness of his childhood.

Slumped there in desolate silence,
I longed to feel what it was he felt,
To know what it was like to be alone,
Alone like he was.

Even now, I long for him to live.

Natalie Kerr (12)
Verdin High School

The Time Traveller

Singing about his childhood,
Like a bird in the sky,
His face, gloomy-eyed, but
always grinning in the sunshine.
His voice, deep and comforting.

Whenever he slept, he dreamt
about 'Silky', he called
out in his dream.

But I was glad he was there
only through him, could I see
and hear the pit children calling.

His clothes, all tattered and torn,
the same every day, his brown
pants and his dirty green T-shirt.

He knew and spoke about
the work from the pit children
as if he was there.

Darkness shone in his eyes,
as he sang the
pit songs aloud.

Then, hearing the voice
of my grandma, like an
echo through the distance.

Slumped there rocking
in her chair.

I longed for thom
both, Grandpa singing
and Grandma rocking.

Sarah Cuffe (12)
Verdin High School

The Time Traveller

Singing about life in the pits,
Like a gramophone stuck in the past,
However, I was glad to hear his stories,
Only through him could I relive the excitement of the mines.

His face round and wrinkled like a ripened peach,
The darkness of the pits shone through his eyes,
His voice croaky from the ancient dust on his chest,
His clothes battered and worn-out.

Whenever he smiled, the world seemed a better place,
He knew the love I felt for him,
He gave me a special love,
One I can't describe.

Then hearing him mumble in his sleep,
Lying in his bed alone in his dream world,
I longed for his voice like a gramophone stuck in the past,
To break the awkward silence of the family,
For him to burst into song and skip around the room.

But never again, only in my sleep, will I see him.

Ben Jackson (13)
Verdin High School

The Time Traveller

Singing about the songs of the pit,
Like an old music box slightly out of tune.
His face looked like the rough bark of a tree,
His voice, as soft as Grandma's.

Whenever Grandpa sleeps, he sighs and whispers,
But I am just glad to hear him breathe,
All day, he lives in his memories,
Telling stories for his fight for survival.

Grandpa knew all the dangers of the pit,
His mind lived in its dark, winding tunnels.
Reflection shone in his eyes of the deep, dark past,
Then I'd hear him mumble his great sadness.

Always slumped there, searching his past,
I longed for his kindness and love.
I wish to break his meaningless stare,
To burst into his thoughts, so I take his hand.

Robert Lally (12)
Verdin High School

The Time Traveller

Singing about the dark, gaseous pits,
Like a howling wolf in a forest,
His moustache stained with nicotine,
His voice ancient as the pit.

He was driven into the pit
Like I was driven to the game called Death,
This caused his stunted back to creak and crack,
But I was glad that he survived the pits.

His clothes never changed,
His eyes endless with memories whenever I looked into them,
Slumped there in the wooden rocking chair, silently smoking cigarettes,
Then hearing his croaky voice call, I immediately reacted.

He could see that I was tempted to play the game called Death,
Although now he has experienced it,
I wish for my grandpa to come back,
To break the restrictions of my love,
To burst into his arms once again.

Matthew Bailey (12)
Verdin High School

THE TIME TRAVELLER

Singing his ancient pit songs
Like my grandad does
His face had a smile spread across it
His voice deep and hoarse

He dreamt of Silky, the little pit boy
In the night he would shout
Wanting to capture the little ghost
'After him,' he would cry out

But I was glad he was there
Only through him could I travel the past
His clothes did not matter to him
A trunk of them would last

He knew of the children
He knew of the song
'When I was young and in me prime, eh aye, I could hew,'
He sang it for so long

Then hearing the door close tightly shut
Slumped there on my floor
I longed for his fingers to run through my hair
For him to run through my door

To burst through the door like a super hero
I sat there on my bed
None of his songs to be sung again
As he would soon be dead.

Clare Whalley (12)
Verdin High School

The Grandad Of All

Singing towards the setting sun,
Wishing once again he was young,
His eyes and mouth, wrinkled and old,
He sounded as if he had no tongue.

What he dreams at night is of things
That I will never know,
Yet for some reason, I think it's about
The pits, where I want to go.

When he looked around all blankly,
Slumped on his wooden chair,
His memory being taken away,
As he looked into nowhere.

Then he looks around and remembers
About some little things,
Maybe a story, a poem, a friend,
Or a song he used to sing.

Just one trunk of clothes and souvenirs,
Is all he had to bring,
The only thing of worth to him
Was his helmet or wedding ring.

Above his bed is a shelf
With a pitman's helmet and a lamp,
And if he gave me both of these things,
It would be too much to ever thank.

Andrew Todd (12)
Verdin High School

The Time Traveller

The emptiness of his eyes reflected,
The sadness and the darkness of the pits,
He sang about the children of the past,
And how they dropped into the blackness,
Never knowing if they would see golden sunlight again . . .

The smile he wore was torn,
Like the few clothes he had,
Like the cheery personality he tried to put on,
When he told tales of the deep, dark pit children,
Who never knew if they would see golden sunlight again . . .

He mourned for his wife whenever he saw,
The fading photo of the couple,
Fading like his memory,
Fading like the light as the children crawled deeper,
Never knowing if they would see golden sunlight again . . .

I longed for his tales of the days in the pits,
But I knew one day they would have to go,
The tales would die as Grandpa would,
Never calling out in the night,
Never knowing if he would see golden sunlight again . . .

'Silky' he'd call after the blond boy in the corner,
'Silky' he'd call as the silver moonlight flowed through the curtains,
His mind was a labyrinth of mysteries,
Of his dark times in the Stoneygate pits,
When he wondered if he would ever see golden sunlight again . . .

He shifted in and out of his grave,
And then death . . . he was gone! Without knowing or feeling,
Anything at all,
Never to see the golden sunlight again . . . ever!

Dale Ollier (12)
Verdin High School

THE TIME TRAVELLER

I died for you Grandpa,
Why've you got your beard?
Is it to do with your scruffy clothes?
Is it something that you feared?

I died for you Grandpa,
When you walked in my room,
It was filled with sunshine.
Is it like that in your tomb?

I died for you Grandpa,
On occasion more than once.
If I'd said I love you,
What would have been your response?

I died for you Grandpa,
With the blade of that knife.
I just wanted to know
Why you treasured life.

I died for you Grandpa,
By John Askew's side.
I know you didn't like his dad,
I'm sorry that I lied.

I died for you Grandpa
And as you trailed away,
I was upset to see
Your thin, frail hair turn grey.

You died for me Grandpa,
You are with Grandma now.
But I learnt how to love,
By you showing me how.

Lauren Leech (12)
Verdin High School

THE TIME TRAVELLER

Singing about the mines, his past
Like a child from his memories
His face rough and cracked like a tree
His voice cold and gravely like the sounds of the pits.

Whenever he slept, he whispered for Grandma to be returned to his side.
But I was glad of his love for me
Only through him could I understand the pits, his life.

His clothes worn with memories of Grandma, the mines.
Grandpa knew the meaning of loneliness and emptiness.
He was blank some days, like he was remembering, or forgetting.

His eyes were the mines, deep black
Then hearing a voice or a cry, he would return to us.
Slumped there in his bed, he relived his past.

I long for his stories, his songs and smile
To break the silence of this room,
To burst like a tree from my heart
Only now can I be grateful for his love.

Sara Hough (12)
Verdin High School

The Time Traveller

Singing the old pit songs,
'Wisht, lads, had yer gobs,
An I'll tell yez an aafull story . . . '
Like he was down there now.

His face was scarred from the hard work
and determination he put into his job.
His voice croaked with old age.

Whenever he was with me, he lit up my life
and I put on a beaming smile for him.

But I was glad of his company
and the love that he cherished for me.
Only through him could I relive
what he went through down the pit.

His clothes were not important to him.
He knew about the game called Death.
I was driven to play it.
In his eyes was Silky, who he had longed to catch.

You could hear the chipping of the rocks.
I was almost down there with him.

Slumped there on my bed, I longed for his pit songs
and the smile that lit up my bedroom.

Daniel Larkin (13)
Verdin High School

THE TIME TRAVELLER

Singing about the pit,
His twisted body entered,
Like an old, dying tree,
His face old, with holes instead of teeth, filled with happiness.

Wrinkles hung off his face,
His twig-like legs struggling for balance,
His hair as grey as an elephant's back,
His fingers brittle and crooked.

Whenever he entered I was happy to see him,
Whenever he left I was sad to see him go.
I loved my grandpa so much,
I am glad I entered his life.

His clothes were old and dull,
He was happy with his life's achievements.
Every time I saw him his eyes were like a deep, dark tunnel
of never-ending sadness.
He knew he would die sooner or later.

I wanted him to go to a happier place,
Yet I wanted him to stay.
I died for you, Grandpa; I died for you, Grandpa,
In the game called Death.

I had to face the truth,
There was no light at the end of the tunnel,
No one could help him, he was sick,
His life had been so long and happy, but every story
must have an ending.

I longed for him to be well again,
To mend death's door,
To go back in time to when he was young,
So we could be best friends.

Peter Wheller (12)
Verdin High School

THE TIME TRAVELLER

Singing about the pits he walked in
Like a lost child and sat down,
His face scarred from an old pit accident,
His voice rough like the ammonite he once gave to me.

Whenever he slept he called out furiously,
Dreaming of Silky,
A boy he could see from the past.

But I was glad of his tales,
Only through him could I picture the past.
His clothes were of no interest to him,
He knew that only his memories were of value to him now.

He was lonely, he needed friends,
Images of Grandma flickered in his dark and tender eyes.
Then, hearing the axes strike again,
He returned to his pit, his world of darkness
And I longed for him to speak of his childhood once more,
To break the restrictions of my reality,
To burst like a bubble of joy into my life again.

Lois Lancaster (12)
Verdin High School

The Time Traveller

Singing the old pit songs,
Like all the birds of the world,
His voice was like the coo of a dove,
Whenever he sang, it lit me up with glee.

His face was as soft and as gentle as feathers,
His clothes were always the same,
He was twisted from working in the ancient pit,
His eyes were deep and empty.

Only through him could I see Silky,
But I was glad he told me the stories.
I longed for more of the strange pit stories,
To break the sadness going through me,
To burst like all the loving memories cramped in his head.

He knew everything you needed to know about the pits,
Slumped there in the deckchair in the garden,
Then hearing his moans and groans,
He'd leave us.

He would drift off into a world of his own,
Leaving us scared and worried.
I'd wish to hear another of his pit songs,
But now all I have are the loving memories cramped in my head.

Dean Ashmore (12)
Verdin High School

THE TIME TRAVELLER

Singing about his time in the pit
Like an old time traveller
His face strained with knowledge
His voice lined with the pit dust

Whenever he entered the house
It was transformed into the pit
The now coal-filled house
Was a haven for ancient songs and stories

But I was glad of his stories
Only through him
Could I relive his experience in the pit

His clothes were not those of a materialist
He knew he was to follow his wife soon
He was fading away with every moment that passed
The white in his eyes seemed to be covering them
Like ivy on an old oak

Then hearing the snoring stop
Slumped there in his padded grave
I longed for him to call out from his endless dream
To break the silence of the night
To burst like a flower from its bud.

Sam Duncalf (12)
Verdin High School

THE TIME TRAVELLER

Singing about the pits,
Like an old tree rustling in the wind,
His voice breaking like a twig,
Flickering like an old record,
Drifting into daydreams of the pit,
I longed for his songs of the pit.

I was glad of his tales of the pit,
Only through him could I relive his adventures of the past,
He knew things most would never know,
Whenever he came, the old pits entered the room,
I see in his eyes the cold pits and Silky dancing,
He's just slumped there in the darkness of the pits.

His face pale and wrinkled from lack of sun,
Then hearing him shout in his dreams,
His clothes were not important to him,
His face occasionally flickered with happiness.

His dreams would burst with cries of his childhood,
Then hearing him shout in his dreams,
He may soon be gone,
But he will be remembered forever.

Paul Smith (12)
Verdin High School

THE TIME TRAVELLER

Singing about the ancient pit songs,
Like a crooked, old fool on the radio,
His face as pale as a plump, ripened peach,
His voice as rough and croaky as an old frog,
His clothes still smell of the pits he once worked in,
His eyes full of unknown secrets and riddles.

Whenever he told me the stories of the past, the tales and the songs,
I knew these things could never last,
But I was glad of his stories, his tales and his songs,
Only through him could I break the border between present and past,
He knew the mysteries of the ancient,
He was my saviour, my champion, my hero.

Then, hearing Grandpa cry, 'Silky,' from his room,
Slumped there in his enormous-looking bed,
I longed to know the secret unknown mysteries of the past,
To break the silence of the room,
To burst the balloon of unawareness I didn't know existed.

All that I have left to say is:
'I miss you Grandpa.'

Natalie Roughsedge (12)
Verdin High School

THE TIME TRAVELLER

Singing the ancient pit songs he strolled in
Like a child from the past;
His face full with the yearning for Grandma.

His voice was gravelly,
Like the sound of children's shoes in the pit,
Whenever he spoke, my imagination ran wild.

I was glad of him for opening my eyes,
Only through him
Could I see through the shadows of the pits.

He knew about the empty feeling of loneliness
And longed for a partner in life.

His eyes were filled with the phosphoric glow of the pits,
Hearing the pit children's voices brought back memories.

Slumped there in a perpetual sleep,
I was filled with a desire for his stories once again.
For him to break the barrier between me and the morose, sombre pits,
To burst like the rays of sunlight into the depth of my imagination.

Corinne Kinvig (12)
Verdin High School

THE TIME TRAVELLER

His face old and wrinkled,
But bursting out with a beaming smile,
His voice croaky and stiff.

The clothes were the same as the weeks,
Tatty and dirty, frayed, with holes.

But I was glad of his company,
His strong smell of the outside world,
Only through him could I see beyond my four walls.

Singing about his dreams of Silky,
Like a bird whistling,
Whenever he came, he seemed to light up the room,
Talking proudly about his memorable pit stories.

He knew what he wanted out of life,
Peace and love, not material things.

My grandpa was a calm person,
Swinging his arms and singing to the sun.
Slumped there in our own little world,
        No worries.

Adele Lafferty (12)
Verdin High School

THE TIME TRAVELLER

Singing about the chill in the pit,
Like a bird suddenly realising how he could sing,
His face darkened from the coal he had hit,
His voice cracked like the axe he'd used.

'When I was young . . . '

Whenever he was at my side,
I was glad he was still alive,
Only through him could I be free,
From what death made of me.

'When I was young . . . '

His clothes a mess,
But he couldn't care less,
He was the light,
From the pits of his night.

'When I was young . . . '

Then hearing his tales,
Slumping face, very pale,
I longed for his life to go on and on,
To break the death and for his song
To be young and in its prime.

Sam Gunn (12)
Verdin High School

THE SURVIVAL OF HOPE

Through the darkness filled with hate and the
treachery and lies . . .
Through the dirt and dangerous creatures that
viciously
fly . . .
Through the dreams that carried no hope
Through the hope that carried no trust
Through the trust on which we depend be filled
with deceit, danger and lust
But still flies a tiny being from which light can't
escape
And that the wings that carry it protect it from
its fate
And that the tiny hopes inside it fly strong
through smoke-filled air
That will suffocate it into our world of suffering,
fear and despair.

Khadeeja Hussain (13)
Wilmslow High School

THE RIVER

Shimmering along a bumpy bed,
Mirroring my movements as I follow its winding trail,
Never ending, always moving,
Amaze me? It could never fail.

Washing away my worries,
Putting a smile on my face,
Flowing towards a sparkling sea,
At a gentle but meandering pace.

Katherine Hull
Wilmslow High School